HUGO ORTEGA'S

# Street Food
## of MEXICO

**bright sky press**
HOUSTON, TEXAS

2365 Rice Boulevard, Suite 202, Houston, Texas 77005

10  9  8  7  6  5  4  3

Library of Congress Cataloging-in-Publication Data

Ortega, Hugo, 1965-
Hugo Ortega's street food of Mexico / Hugo Ortega with Ruben Ortega.
p. cm.
ISBN 978-1-936474-73-8
1. Street food--Mexico. 2. Cooking, Mexican. I. Ortega, Ruben, 1971- II.
Title.

TX716.M4O77 2012
641.5972--dc23                    2012017063

Design, Wyn Bomar Design
Project Editor, Julia Pemberton Hellums
Recipe Testing and Translation, Cristina Ramírez Vargas

Bright Sky Press Creative Director, Ellen Peeples Cregan
Bright Sky Press Editorial Director, Lucy Herring Chambers

Printed in Canada through Friesens

# HUGO ORTEGA'S

# Street Food
# of MEXICO

## HUGO ORTEGA with Ruben Ortega

### photographs by Penny De Los Santos

bright sky press
HOUSTON, TEXAS

To my daughter, Sophia, who is my inspiration

and of whom I am immensely proud.

To my wife, Tracy, who believed in me and paved the way

for me to achieve things I never thought that I could.

— HUGO ORTEGA —


To my wife, Priscila, and my *hermoso hijo*, my son, Mateo: thank you for

believing in me and giving me the courage to keep the dream alive.

— RUBEN ORTEGA—


We would also like to dedicate this book to the women of our

family who loved us unconditionally, kept our family together

and taught us to honor Mexican customs and traditions.


To our *abuelita* Delia who taught us to respect and love nature.

To our *abuelita* Oliva, our family treasure, who built

our confidence with her encouraging words.


To our mother, Zoila, who tirelessly dedicated her life to raising

eight children and instilled in us our love of cooking.


To our sisters, Alma, Guadalupe and twins Gloriela

and Veronica who love us and have always tried, albeit

unsuccessfully at times, to keep us on the right track.

— HUGO AND RUBEN ORTEGA —

Our *abuelita* Delia with Sophia

June 2002, Progreso, Mexico

# CONTENTS

**6:00 a.m., Mexico City,** and the streets are alive with millions of people, all making their way through the city: to work, to school, to the market. This is one of the world's largest and most populated areas. Life moves at a fast pace in this bustling modern city, yet old world Mexico is everywhere, especially in the air. Aromas of "street food" fill every city block. At any corner, at any time of day, you will find something delicious to eat: fresh *jugos* and *atoles*, *pan dulce*, *tacos* and *tortas*. *Mercados* filled with an endless variety of food stalls offer every dish imaginable. The food is as varied as the Mexican people themselves, with dishes from every region and every indigenous culture of the country. People from all over migrate to Mexico City to find work as vendors, and they bring an important taste of their home. Street food is integral to the city and to the Mexican way of life. It nourishes city-dwellers as well as those who have made lengthy treks from the surrounding countryside and villages. It is "fast food" at its finest, because the only thing fast about it is how it is served.

Mexican street food is actually "slow food," prepared in someone's home kitchen with little to no shortcuts from family recipes handed down through the ages. The food is cooked all through the night on the outskirts of the towns and villages, in kitchen ovens or in deep earthen pits, and brought into city and town centers each morning. It feeds residents and workers quickly and efficiently and is a means by which thousands of Mexicans support their families. Rich with tradition and heritage, street food is the purest form of true, authentic Mexican cuisine. What chefs espouse today — grow local, cook local — is nothing new for Mexican cooks. This is how they have been preparing food for centuries.

I was born in Mexico City, the oldest of eight children. I grew up in its worst slums. As it does for all Mexicans, food played an important role in our lives. So much of our heritage is shared through food and gathering for meals. Sometimes we had enough, and other times not, and so, like many in my homeland, I began working at a very young age to help support my family. As a little boy, I would often get up at 4:00 a.m. to put freshly made flan onto trays and take the bus into town to sell them at the *mercado*. This was my first job in the food business. My grandfather was a great carpenter. He made special shoeshine kits for each of my cousins and me, with our initials carved on the front. We would load up our kits and head out to the busy streets together every day. My goal was simple: to make enough money so that I could buy a *huarache,* my favorite food, from the stall on the corner opposite from where we worked. I would shine a couple of pairs of shoes and run to ask my cousin, "Do I have enough?" "No, you need more," he would tell me, over and over. To be honest, I was terrible at the job, but somehow I would eventually earn enough to buy my breakfast. The flavors and aroma of that well-earned meal are still clear in my memory today, and it is one of the reasons why I want to celebrate the foods of the streets, of my Mexican childhood, of these unique culinary traditions.

When I was around ten, we moved to the home of my grandparents in Puebla. It was a sad time for me. Although we lived on my mother's family's property with many relatives, I dreamed of being back in the city with its liveliness and excitement — it was my comfort zone. Eventually, I came to enjoy life in Puebla, and it was during

this time that I learned the importance of growing and sourcing my food. We had a large garden where we grew corn, tomatoes, squashes, green beans, peanuts and watermelons. Our small working farm included cows, pigs, turkeys, chickens and goats, among other animals. The richness of the love I feel for cooking goes back to time spent preparing food with my mother and grandmother in the mountains of Puebla. They taught me the fundamentals of Mexican cooking and also their own special touches. They were both traditional cooks, preparing all the dishes typical of the area in the only way they knew how — over wood-burning fires, wrapped in corn husks, everything from scratch. Corn was ground fresh every day for *tortillas*; *nopales* (cactus paddles) were cleaned and charred over a wood fire; and there was always a pot of beans simmering. We grew and raised as much of our food as possible. In the countryside, everything is about seasonality and rain — Mother Nature determines what you prepare.

When I was fourteen, we moved back to Mexico City and my father opened a grocery store. He made all of the shelves and the long wooden counter by hand. I worked in the store, but I was not a very good *comerciante*, merchant. I loved soccer too much and would often leave the shoppers to take care of themselves while I played, much to the dismay of my father. One of my cousins was living in Houston, Texas, and I read a letter that he had sent back to his mother. Everything sounded wonderful,

and it opened my eyes to new opportunities. After several failed attempts, in 1984, at age seventeen, I arrived in Houston knowing just one person. I had no money, no job, only the determination to make a better life for myself.

It was a hard transition for me — I missed the traditions and the familiar way of living in Mexico. The food and people in Texas were so different, and I didn't speak English. Houston at that time was going through an "oil bust," and the city was not doing well. I shared an apartment with several friends and was happy to find my first job, as a dishwasher. While the pay was meager, I grabbed at the opportunity to learn the fundamentals of the restaurant business and find contacts to improve my English.

I worked as a busboy during the day and cleaned the floors in office buildings at night to supplement my income. I was fortunate to have two steady-paying jobs, but then everything changed. My roommates decided to move to California and then, with an unexpected turn of bad luck, I lost my jobs. I was homeless and jobless. It was the worst time of my life.

"*¿Quieres lavar platos?*" — "Do you want to wash dishes?" — a friend asked me when we were playing soccer in the park. He took me to Backstreet Cafe and introduced me to the owner, Tracy Vaught. It was here that the greatest opportunity of my life came. I remember Tracy's voice like it was yesterday. She offered me a job, I accepted, and we shook hands. I started work that afternoon.

I worked very hard, and my love for cooking often took me into the kitchen to watch the chef, who would show me techniques and teach me recipes. I was soon given a position on the kitchen line. Tracy offered to help me enroll in the Culinary Arts Program at Houston Community College. I was achieving things that exceeded my dreams.

I received a culinary degree in 1992 and became chef, then executive chef, of Backstreet Cafe, where I had once been dishwasher. Along the way, Tracy and I fell in love and were married. Through the years, Tracy would suggest going out for Mexican food. Once there, I would always tell her, "This is not Mexican food." It was different from the food that I grew up preparing and eating. What is often served in Mexican restaurants in Texas is Mexican-American, Southwestern or Tex-Mex. While it can be delicious, it is not authentic. The idea of Hugo's restaurant started as a drive from within me to create a place that represented the traditional food of my country.

Before I opened Hugo's, my father, Ruben and I made a culinary pilgrimage to Mexico. Our journey took us some 4,000 miles around Mexico, along the east and west coasts and across the interior — eating, meeting the local cooks and rediscovering the remarkable history, textures, flavors and diversity found throughout this beautiful, rugged land. During this journey, I found inspiration and a renewed passion for the bounties found in Mexico and its cuisine, as well as a recognition that the street food of Mexico is in many ways the most authentic record of Mexico's culinary traditions. Mexican food is extremely diverse — as light and fresh as a seafood cocktail prepared by fishermen on the beach; as deep and complex as *moles* from

Oaxaca made with an astounding number of ingredients; and as earthy as the simplest homemade corn *tortilla*. *Comerciantes* in the streets serve it in its truest, purest forms.

My younger brother, Ruben, has been side-by-side with me on these travels and in my restaurants. As executive pastry chef, he prepares sweet works of art, both creative and traditional desserts, featured in the *Dulces* and *Bebidas* chapters of this book. We both share a deep love of our homeland, its culture and traditions. We express it the only way we know how: through our cooking.

Mexican food is my heritage and my passion. I am no more of an expert on Mexican cuisine than the tens of thousands of home cooks who prepare and serve the street food of Mexico. I am simply cooking the food that I love, from my heart. My food memories are rich with the vivid flavors of my Mexican childhood and inspired by the classical training of my culinary education and my life in the diverse city of Houston. Although I left Mexico as a teenager, I always carried Mexico in my heart. My goal is to share my knowledge and my love for the rich heritage of true Mexican cuisine and Mexican street food, both here and in my restaurant kitchen. I want you to experience Mexico as you travel through these pages, and to be inspired to prepare these recipes for your family and friends. I share these dishes and stories as a tribute to the cuisine of my native land and, most importantly, to its people, who keep its traditions alive, one dish at a time. When I cook, I cook for them.

**Notes From My Mexican Kitchen:** Like any other part of the world, life in Mexico has become busier, preventing people from spending hours preparing meals. But, a stop at a nearby *taco*, *torta* or *antojito* stand creates a connection. Street vendors are a link to a culinary world many people do not have the opportunity to fully experience. Thanks to local street stands, they can visit their favorite vendors for a home-cooked breakfast, lunch and/ or pre-dinner snack away from home. The wonderful thing about Mexican street food is that because vendors keep traditions, people are able to enjoy food prepared the way their mothers or even grandmothers used to make it. This food is from the people, for the people.

For this cookbook, I tested and prepared the following recipes in my restaurant kitchen, surrounded by people I work with every day who are truly experts in this cuisine. My kitchen brigade represents many parts of Mexico — Oaxaca, Puebla, Veracruz and the northern parts near the border. It was a great experience to share the making of this cookbook with the people who I wanted to represent in my recipes. I asked and received input from everyone on my kitchen staff each step of the way. I recall one occasion when we were testing a particular recipe, one of my favorites as well as very popular among my fellow cooks — *taquitos de cabeza*. In Mexico, it is customary for *taco* stand vendors to roast a whole animal, usually the pig, and offer *taquitos* from different cuts of the animal, one being the *cabeza*, or head. When the pig's head came out of the oven, all of my cooks formed a line with a small *tortilla* in hand ready to eat a *taquito* from their favorite cut of the pig's head. As they served themselves, I heard many memories. It was an inspiring day. Everybody had something to say, a story to share. It became very important to me to keep to tradition in these recipes and to incorporate the cooking methods that I remember from my childhood and those that I heard from the memories shared by the experts of my Mexican kitchen.

I invite you to enter the world of Mexican street food, filled with vibrant ingredients, deep-rooted traditions and authentic people. My life in the kitchen has this richness: it is a world I was able to enter and never leave. I have surrounded myself with wonderful people, strong and wise, who have taught me so much along the way.

To recreate the authenticity of Mexican street food a few things are important to consider before you begin. Keep in mind that although it is street food, it is far from being fast food. It is traditional home-cooked food that can be eaten on the go.

## Make-Ahead Instructions and Staples

It comes naturally for me to do things from scratch. It is how I learned to cook growing up in my grandmother's kitchen. I have offered make-ahead instructions here to cut down on prep time, but at the same time I have tried to stick to the cooking methods and procedures street vendors practice to this day. Vendors prepare these items in episodes — sometimes over a period of a couple of days — as they need to marinate, slow-roast the food, pack it up and take it to their carts or stands at nearby *mercados* to sell. In many of the recipes, marinating and roasting can be done up to three days ahead and the food can be reheated before serving.

It is helpful to keep a few homemade staples on hand. For example, *refritos* (page 132), refried beans, are always in my refrigerator as they are frequently an ingredient in Mexican street food. They act as a spread in *tortas*, a filling in *tacos* or a simple side for any meal. They can be made up to three days in advance and stored in the refrigerator. *Chiles curtidos* (page 128), pickled peppers, are great to top *tacos* or to give an authentic kick to a favorite *torta*. They can be prepared and refrigerated for several weeks. I stock my refrigerator with fresh Mexican ingredients like *serrano* peppers, *tomatillos*, cilantro and avocado, all great ingredients to whip up a quick *salsa* when needed. Many of the garnishes and *salsas* found in *Salsas*, Chapter 3, can be prepared up to three days in advance or in large quantities as they go well with many dishes. Cool and store according to directions on page 115. Fresh ingredients can serve as garnishes as well: thinly sliced radishes, chopped cilantro or white onion, lime wedges, crumbled *queso fresco* and more. Feel free to substitute with what you have on hand in any of the following recipes.

## Essential Fresh and Dry Pantry Ingredients

Traditional Mexican street food could not be possible without authentic Mexican ingredients, which are identified in italics here. You will find important information about many of these ingredients in the Glossary section (page 246-250). Living in Texas, I am privileged to have a Mexican grocery store close by where authentic Mexican ingredients are readily available. I invite you to seek out a store like this in your town or city. Mexican spices, produce, dairy and pantry items are available at these stores, which are fun places to visit and explore. Some ingredients have found their way to the Hispanic/ethnic foods aisle in the majority of large supermarkets. In some urban communities, like Houston, Mexican farmers markets exist and are filled with delicious, beautiful Mexican produce, aromatic herbs as well as traditional dry spices.

*Masa* is one of the essential ingredients needed to recreate traditional Mexican street food. There are a few types, all of which are available at selective Mexican grocery stores with a *tortillería*, tortilla-making section, in-house. Fresh *masa* is a dough-like substance made from grinding corn kernels, or *maíz*, which has been simmered in slaked lime and hulled. Fresh *masa para tamales* is similar to the previously mentioned *masa* but has a coarser texture, adequate for making *tamales*. It is sometimes found in 5-pound plastic bags in the refrigerators in Mexican grocery stores. For easier-to-find alternatives, see the instructions in the *masa* master recipe on page 24.

Lard, or *manteca*, is another ingredient that is very traditional but might cause you some hesitation. It is rendered and clarified pork fat, which is used in traditional Mexican cuisine. Although using lard will give a more authentic street flavor, feel free to substitute with corn oil as well as olive oil. However, use corn oil for frying as it has a higher smoking point.

Mexican cheeses are essential ingredients for making authentic *tortas, tacos* and *antojitos*. They can be found in the dairy section in Mexican grocery stores or the imported cheese section in gourmet stores. One cheese that is particularly important to find is *quesillo* or *queso Oaxaca*, a mild, semi-hard thread cheese from Oaxaca, in southern Mexico. It is sold in small yarn-like rounds.

## Special Equipment

A few pieces of special equipment will be important for authentically replicating these recipes: a *comal*, a *tortilla* press and a cast iron skillet. This equipment can be purchased at Mexican grocery stores, farmers markets or online. When looking at the many choices out there, I suggest investing in equipment made with cast iron, a durable, strong material that will last years if you care for it properly. The following recipes were prepared, tested and re-tested using a cast iron *comal* as well as a skillet.

A *comal* can take many forms. It is seen in some *mercados*, or markets, as the traditional shallow oval, clay-made pot with a slight concave center. Alternatively, it is commonly seen in a *tianguis*, a nomadic open-air market that sets up in different locations on different days, as simply a round, sheet of metal that is placed over coals to provide a cooking surface. For the home cook, a *comal* can be a shallow, concave oval made of carbon steel, aluminum or cast iron. A round or oval cast iron griddle or skillet can also be used as a substitute.

A *tortilla* press can be as practical or traditional as you like. Large wooden presses are still commonly used in Mexico and can be found in artisanal shops in the United States. If you find one, purchase it, as these make wonderful kitchen treasures. For the home-cook, a *tortilla* press comes in two basic sizes — 6 or 8 inches in diameter — and can be made of either cast iron or shiny aluminum.

Finally, it is important to know your equipment. As I crafted these recipes for your use at home, I used my trusty old cast iron skillet with a wooden handle. It is a great instrument to cook, simmer, sear, toast spices and roast peppers, as mentioned in the *Salsas* chapter. It is a great investment and an alternative for a *comal*. Despite the burnt handle, my skillet is still in great condition. Remember to follow the seasoning and care instructions on the package when purchasing any special equipment.

I have collected these tips and suggestions throughout the years — from working side by side with my fellow cooks, in my travels and from the women in my family. I hope they help you replicate the authenticity of Mexican street food in the comfort of your own home. As you invest your time in replicating these wonderful dishes, I invite you to enjoy them as they are in Mexico, surrounded by friends and family.

Antojitos

**Antojitos** are a staple of the Mexican street food menu — small *masa* snacks to tide you over until dinner or enjoy as a feel-good treat. Each *antojito* changes name region by region. For example, *pellizcadas* are *masa* tartlets with a pinched rim but are also known as *picadas* in parts of Veracruz, *memelas* in Oaxaca and *sopes* in Jalisco. All of them share the commonality of the pinched ridge but each has a different depth to hold their topping ingredients. The photographs on the next two pages show just a sample of the variety of shapes and toppings with which these *masa*-based snacks can be made. Despite the region, size or shape, *antojitos* are all made with the same primary ingredient: *masa* (page 24).

This chapter offers my recipes for traditional street food *antojitos*. It is *comida casera*, or home-cooked food, prepared to be eaten on the go. Vendors spend many hours preparing the stews, roasting the meats, and making the *masa* bases in their home kitchens the night before. Everything is then packed into baskets and transported to their street stall or street corner to serve their customers the next day.

When making the *masa* bases for these recipes in your kitchen, place them, after shaping, on a sheet pan lined with parchment paper, cover with additional parchment and wrap tightly with plastic wrap. Refrigerate them until you are ready to cook and assemble them for serving. Although the majority of these *antojitos* can be shaped and stuffed the previous day, they should be eaten soon after they are panfried in order to experience the full dimension of flavors.

**Masa** is the backbone of Mexican cooking, as it symbolizes the roots, tradition and people of Mexico. Making *masa* is a long and tedious process that usually falls in the hands of the experts of Mexican cooking — the women. The main ingredient is the *maíz*, or corn — blue, white, yellow, purple and red. It is simmered in water and slaked lime long enough for the hulls to peel off easily. The corn is then drained and rinsed — this stage is called *nixtamal*. Finally, it is put through a mill and ground into a dough-like substance which is called fresh *masa*. Before there were mills, women used to mill the corn on a three-legged stone mortar called a *metate* with a pestle, or *mano*.

Fresh *masa* is available in selective Mexican grocery stores, especially those with a *tortillería* in-house. I highly recommend trying it if you have a local source in your community. Adjust the consistency by adding a small amount of water — about ¼ cup water per 1 pound fresh *masa* — to acquire a soft dough-like texture. If it is unavailable to you, *masa harina* or instant corn *masa* flour mix can be found in the Hispanic/ethnic foods aisle in supermarkets — a powdery mixture made up of ground, cooked corn kernels that have been dried and processed, or *nixtamalizado*.

It can be confusing when you look at the different kinds of packaged corn *masa* mixes in the store. For the recipes in this chapter, buy "instant corn *masa* mix for *tortillas*, *quesadillas*, *pupusas*, *huaraches*, *empanadas*, *gorditas* and *sopes*." All of these uses will be listed on the bag. It can be made out of white or yellow corn. Be sure not to confuse *masa* mix with flour for *tortillas*.

When recipes call for fresh *masa*, you can use this recipe as an alternative.

[ MASTER RECIPE ]
..........................................................................................................................

**Recipe for 1 pound *masa* made with store-bought mix:**
    **2 cups instant corn *masa* flour (yellow or white)**
    **¼ teaspoon kosher salt**

Place *masa* flour, salt and 1 ¼ cups water in a bowl and mix together until a homogenized and smooth dough forms, about 2 minutes. Cover with a moistened clean kitchen towel until ready to use, or store in the refrigerator up to a day covered with parchment paper then wrapped in plastic. This will prevent it from drying out and acquiring a crust.

# Tlacoyos
## Masa Cakes Stuffed *with* Refried Beans | *Makes 4-8 servings*

*Tlacoyos* are *masa* cakes stuffed with refried beans — pinto or black. They are usually prepared the night before and the ladies (page 18-19) pack them in baskets to sell the next day. If making ahead, place the raw *tlacoyos* on a sheet pan lined with a piece of parchment paper; cover with another piece of parchment paper and plastic wrap. Cook on a hot *comal* right before serving. The *papas, champiñones y acelgas* taco filling (page 96) is another great vegetarian option that can be used as a topping for this recipe.

### For the *salsa*:

- 8 tomatoes, roasted
- ½ cup finely chopped white onion
- 3 whole *serrano* peppers, stemmed
- 1 cup *epazote* leaves, loosely packed
- ½ cup olive oil
- 1½ tsp kosher salt

### For the *tlacoyos*:

- 1 lb *masa* (fresh or prepared from mix, page 24)
- ½ cup *refritos* (page 132)
- 1 tbsp corn oil
- 8 *flores de calabaza* (squash blossoms), washed, stemmed
- ½ avocado, peeled, pitted, cubed
- ¼ roasted white onion, optional for garnish

**For the *salsa* (make ahead up to 1 day):** Place tomatoes, white onion, peppers and *epazote* in blender and purée until smooth. Refrigerate covered until ready to use.

Place cast iron skillet over medium heat, add olive oil to skillet and preheat 2 minutes. Add the *salsa* and cook for 2 minutes, stirring constantly. Reduce heat to low and simmer until reduced by a third, about 10 minutes. Add salt.

**For the *tlacoyos* (make ahead up to 1 day):** Divide the *masa* into eight equal *masa* balls; cover with a moistened kitchen towel while working. Using the palm of your hand, flatten each *masa* ball into a patty, about 4 inches in diameter and ¼ inch thick. Place 1 tablespoon *refritos* in the center and enclose the beans inside each patty by rolling it into a cylinder. Place each cylinder on a clean surface and pat down into an oval shape, about ¼ inch thick. Store in refrigerator until ready to cook.

**Before serving:** Place *comal* over low heat, preheat 5 minutes. Drizzle with corn oil and wipe off excess with a paper towel. Working two at a time, place each *tlacoyo* onto the hot *comal* and cook 3 to 5 minutes on each side. Remove from *comal* and top each with 1 squash blossom, ¼ cup of the *salsa*, 1 tablespoon cubed avocado. Garnish with onion, if using.

# Huaraches con nopales y frijoles de olla
## Sandal-Shaped Masa Cakes *with* Diced Cactus Paddles *and* Beans
*Makes 4 servings*

*Huaraches* are oblong *masa* cakes in the shape of a sandal, or "huarache," with a small ridge pinched around the edge. My favorite are those made with blue corn *masa* as they remind me of my childhood. At Hugo's, we make a smaller version of these, *huarachitos*, and offer them as an appetizer. If you are making them for a party, shape the *masa* up to one day ahead and store as directed on page 21. Cook them again in melted lard just before topping and serving.

| | |
|---|---|
| 1 lb *masa* (fresh or prepared from mix, page 24) | 4 *nopales* (cactus paddles), cleaned (page 249) |
| 1 tbsp corn oil | ½ lb *quesillo* or also known as queso Oaxaca |
| 4 tbsp lard, melted | ½ cup *salsa de tomatillo* (page 119) |
| 1 cup *frijoles de olla* (page 132) | |

**For the *huaraches* (make ahead up to 1 day):** Divide the *masa* into four equal *masa* balls; cover with a moistened kitchen towel while working. Roll out each *masa* ball into a cylinder, about 8 inches long and 1 inch thick. Working one at a time, place each cylinder in between two large pieces of parchment paper and lightly press down with the palm of your hand until achieving a long oval *masa* cake of an even ¼ inch thickness.

Place *comal* over low heat, preheat 5 minutes. Drizzle with corn oil and wipe off excess with a paper towel. Cook each *huarache* on the hot *comal* 3 minutes per side. Remove from *comal* and while still hot, pinch a border about ¼ inch deep all around the *huarache*, creating a well. Have a clean, moistened kitchen towel nearby to wet fingers to prevent them from burning. Store *huaraches* according to directions on page 21 until ready to prepare toppings and serve.

**Before serving:** Place *comal* over low heat, preheat 5 minutes. Working one at a time, place each cactus paddle on the hot *comal* and sear, about 6 minutes per side. Place cactus paddles on a clean cutting board and dice.

Working one at a time, drizzle 2 teaspoons melted lard onto the hot *comal* and 1 teaspoon inside the well of each *huarache*, making sure it is evenly coated. Place on the *comal* well-side down and cook until crispy, about 2 minutes. Turn over and crisp the base of the *huarache*, about 2 minutes more. Remove from heat and transfer to a warm platter.

Top each *huarache* with ¼ cup *frijoles de olla*, followed by ½ cup diced *nopales*, a handful of *quesillo* and 2 tablespoons *salsa de tomatillo*.

# Picadas
## Masa Tartlets *with a* Roasted Tomato Sauce | *Makes 4 servings*

*Picadas*, as they are known in Veracruz, are *masa* tartlets, similar to thick *tortillas*, with a pinched border to hold in a pool of sauce. They are known as p*ellizcadas (*which means "pinched" in Spanish) in some parts of Mexico and *memelas* in Oaxaca. The corn *masa* base is the same; however, the toppings change depending on the region. The following recipe was inspired by the *picadas* I have enjoyed on my visits to Veracruz. They are wonderful for breakfast especially when accompanied with a steaming cup of *café lechero* (page 228).

| | |
|---|---|
| 2½ lbs tomatoes, roasted, peeled | 1½ tsp kosher salt |
| 4 garlic cloves, peeled | 1 lb *masa* (fresh or prepared from mix, page 24) |
| 4 dried bay leaves | |
| ⅓ cup corn oil plus 1 tbsp, divided | 1 cup *queso fresco*, crumbled |
| 1 cup finely chopped white onion | |

Place tomatoes, garlic and bay leaves in a blender and purée until smooth. Place a small saucepan over medium heat, add ⅓ cup corn oil to pan and preheat 2 minutes. Add onion and cook until translucent, about 3 minutes. Lower heat to medium and slowly add the tomato purée. Bring sauce to a boil, about 1 minute. Reduce heat to low and allow sauce to simmer for 20 minutes, stirring occasionally. Add the salt. Remove from heat.

Divide the *masa* into eight equal balls; cover with a moistened kitchen towel while working. Using the palm of your hand, flatten each *masa* ball into a thick *tortilla*, about 5 ½ inches in diameter and ¼ inch thick.

Place *comal* over low heat, preheat 5 minutes. Drizzle with remaining corn oil and wipe off excess with a paper towel. Working one at a time, place each thick *tortilla* on the hot *comal* and cook 3 minutes per side. Remove from heat and while still hot, pinch a border about ¼ inch deep all around the edge. Have a clean, moistened kitchen towel nearby to wet fingers to prevent them from burning. Transfer to a warm platter.

Pour ¼ cup of the sauce on each *picada* and evenly sprinkle each one with an equal amount of *queso fresco*.

# Empanadas rellenas de verduras
## Savory Half-Moon Pies Stuffed *with* Mixed Vegetables
### *Makes 4-6 servings*

*Empanadas* are common and versatile half-moon stuffed pies that can be either savory or sweet, *masa* or flour-made. These *empanadas* are stuffed with familiar Mexican vegetables like *calabacitas*, *nopales* and *chayote*. *Chayote* and *calabacitas* belong to the gourd family with melons and squash. They can easily be found along with *nopales* in local Mexican and specialty grocery stores. The great thing about this recipe is that you can substitute with any seasonal vegetables. Keep in mind to cut all the vegetables to a similar size so they cook evenly. These *empanadas* can be shaped, stuffed and refrigerated up to one day ahead, then cooked right before serving.

**For the filling:**
- 5 tbsp olive oil, divided
- ¼ cup finely chopped white onion
- 1 garlic clove, peeled, minced
- 2 lbs tomatoes, roasted, peeled, coarsely chopped
- 1½ tsp kosher salt
- ½ tsp dried Mexican oregano, crumbled

- 1½ cup cubed *calabacita* (Mexican zucchini)
- 1 cup cubed *nopales* (cactus paddles)
- ½ cup each cubed *chayote*, carrot and red potato
- ½ *poblano* pepper, roasted, peeled, seeded, coarsely chopped

**For the *empanadas*:**
- 1 lb *masa* (fresh or prepared from mix, page 24)
- ½ cup *queso Cotija*, crumbled

- 12 fresh *epazote* leaves
- 1 tbsp corn oil

**For the filling:** Place cast iron skillet over medium heat, add 3 tablespoons olive oil to skillet and preheat 2 minutes. Add onion and garlic. Cook for 1 minute, stirring. Lower heat to medium and add tomatoes, salt and oregano. Cook until reduced by half, about 12 minutes, stirring occasionally and breaking up tomatoes with the back of a spoon. Keep sauce warm over low heat while preparing the vegetable mix.

Place sauté pan over medium heat, add remaining olive oil and preheat 1 minute. Add *calabacita* and cook 1 minute until lightly brown. Add *nopales* and cook 1 minute more. Add *chayote*, carrot and red potato and continue to cook 2 minutes. Stir vegetables gently throughout to prevent them from losing their shape. Lastly, stir in *poblano* pepper and cook 1 minute more. Gently add vegetable mix to tomato sauce. Remove from heat and allow mixture to cool at least 20 minutes before stuffing *empanadas*.

**For the *empanadas* (make ahead up to 1 day):** Divide the *masa* into 12 equal balls; cover with a moistened kitchen towel. Working one at a time, place each *masa* ball in a *tortilla* press (page 74). Lightly press into a 4-inch wide *tortilla*. Place 2 tablespoons of filling on one half of the *tortilla*, top with 1 teaspoon *queso Cotija* and 1 *epazote* leaf. Fold the other half circle over the filling to form a half-moon pie. Keep *empanadas* covered with the kitchen towel while working. Store in refrigerator according to directions on page 21.

Place *comal* over low heat, preheat 5 minutes. Drizzle with corn oil and wipe off excess with a paper towel. Place up to three *empanadas* at a time onto the hot *comal* and cook fully, about 8 minutes per side. Place finished *empanadas* on a sheet pan in a warm oven as you work. Serve on a warm platter for a party snack and accompany with *salsa de aguacate* (page 125).

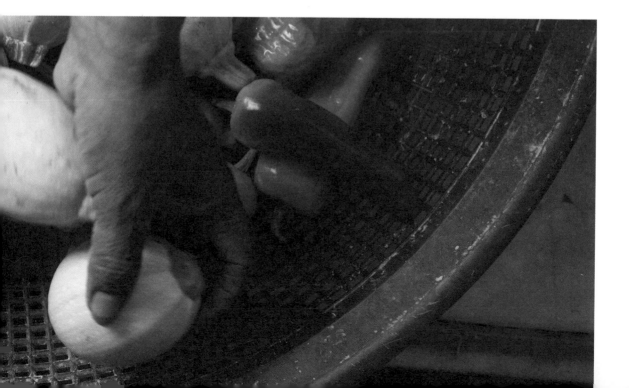

# Empanadas de camarón
## Half-Moon Pies Stuffed *with* Shrimp | *Makes 6 servings*

These *empanadas* were inspired by a recent visit to a seafood market in Mexico City. From far away, we heard what sounded like drums but was actually rolling pins hitting the table as three young men rolled out dough, placed filling in center, formed the *empanada* then fried it, all in a matter of what seemed like seconds (see photo on following page).

**For the dough:**

- 3 cups all-purpose flour
- 1½ tsp kosher salt
- 1 stick (4 oz) unsalted butter, cubed, chilled
- 2 eggs, lightly beaten

**For the filling:**

- ⅓ cup olive oil
- ½ cup finely chopped white onion
- 4 garlic cloves, peeled, minced
- 6 tomatoes, seeded, cut into ½-inch cubes
- 2 dried bay leaves
- 1 tsp dried Mexican oregano, crumbled
- 4 tsp capers, coarsely chopped
- 1 *jalapeño* pepper, seeded and finely chopped
- 3 tbsp distilled white vinegar
- 2 tbsp *salsa inglesa* (Worcestershire sauce)
- 1 lb medium cocktail shrimp, peeled, coarsely chopped

**10 to 12 cups corn oil for frying**

**For the dough:** Place flour, salt, butter, lightly beaten egg and ½ cup ice water in food processor. Pulse until dough begins to form a ball. Transfer onto a piece of plastic, wrap tightly and refrigerate at least 1 hour before using.

**For the filling:** Place large frying pan over medium heat, add olive oil to pan and preheat 2 minutes. Add onion and garlic and cook 3 minutes. Add tomatoes, bay leaves, oregano, capers and *jalapeño* and cook, stirring, 2 minutes. Add vinegar and *salsa inglesa* and cook 2 minutes more. Reduce heat, add shrimp and cook until no longer opaque. Add salt to taste. Transfer mixture to a sheet pan and allow to cool in refrigerator.

**For the *empanadas* (make ahead up to 1 day):** Divide the dough into six equal dough balls. Working one at a time and using a rolling pin, roll each dough ball into circles, about 8 inches in diameter and ⅛ inch thick. Place 2 tablespoons of filling in the center. Lightly brush edges with water, fold one side over mixture and lightly twist and pinch edges to seal. Place raw *empanadas* on parchment-lined tray sprinkled with flour, cover with more parchment paper then plastic wrap. Refrigerate. Fry just before serving.

**Before serving:** Place corn oil in Dutch oven, preheat to 350°F. Working one at a time, deep fry each *empanada* until golden brown, about 3 minutes. Place cooked *empanadas* on paper towels to drain. Serve on a warm platter and accompany with mayonnaise and Valentina® sauce.

# Panuchos
## Thick Tortillas Stuffed *with* Beans and Boiled Eggs Topped *with* Pork
*Makes 4-6 servings*

In the Yucatán, *panuchos* are the area's symbolic version of *gorditas* – thick *tortillas* slit open to have a pouch to stuff and then topped with shredded meat. To make ahead, store stuffed *panuchos* according to directions on page 21 and top with meat just before serving.

**For the pork and *panuchos*:**

| | |
|---|---|
| 1 pork butt (3 lb), bone-in | 1 lb *masa* (fresh or prepared from mix, page 24) |
| 1 tbsp *achiote* paste | |
| 2 tbsp fresh orange juice | ¼ cup lard |
| 2 tbsp fresh lime juice | ½ cup *refritos* (page 132) |
| 2 tsp kosher salt, divided | 4 boiled eggs, thinly sliced |
| 2 large banana leaves | |

**To assemble:**

| | |
|---|---|
| 1 cup beef stock | ½ cup *cebolla en vinagre* (page 128) |
| ¼ cup corn oil | |

**For pork (make ahead up to 2 days):** Preheat oven to 325°F. Place pork butt on a sheet pan and pierce meat with a knife. Place *achiote* paste, orange juice, lime juice and 1 ½ teaspoons salt into blender and purée until smooth. Pour over pork butt, especially in the holes. Completely wrap in banana leaves.

Pour ½ cup of water into a Dutch oven or oven-proof pot, place wrapped pork butt inside. Cover with lid or aluminum foil and place in oven until fork tender, about 4 hours. Add liquid to pot as needed. Remove from oven and allow pork butt to rest for 15 minutes. Remove and discard leaves. Debone and shred meat. Return to pot and store covered in refrigerator.

**For the *panuchos* (make ahead up to 1 day):** Place *masa* on a clean surface and create a well in the center. Place remaining salt and lard into well, and knead into *masa*. Divide into eight equal *masa* balls; cover with a moistened kitchen towel while working. Using the palm of your hand, flatten each *masa* ball into a thick *tortilla*, about 4½ inches in diameter and ¼ inch thick.

Place *comal* over low heat, preheat 5 minutes. Working one at a time, cook each unstuffed *panucho* on the hot *comal*, 2 minutes per side. Remove from heat and allow to cool slightly. Using a sharp knife, make a pocket on one of the edges of each *panucho*. Carefully spread 1 tablespoon *refritos* inside the pocket and add 4 egg slices. Store in refrigerator well wrapped.

**To assemble:** Preheat oven to 325°F. Allow meat to come up to room temperature. Add beef stock to pot, cover and place in oven. Allow to warm up, about 30 minutes.

**Before serving:** Working two at a time, drizzle 1 tablespoon corn oil on the hot *comal*. Cook each *panucho* until crispy, 2 minutes per side. Transfer to a warm platter. Divide pork evenly to top the eight *panuchos*. Garnish each one with 4 slices of *cebolla en vinagre*.

# Salbutes con pato en recado negro
## Thick Tortillas Topped *with* Duck *in a* Black Seasoning Paste
### Makes 4-6 servings

Although it is similar to the *panucho*, the *salbute* is not stuffed and is commonly topped with a traditional Yucatecan turkey dish in a black seasoning paste. I decided to offer a twist and create a recipe using duck, but a 3 ½-pound chicken or a small turkey will work as well.

**For the duck and *salbutes*:**
- 1 whole duck (4 to 5 lb)
- 3½ tsp kosher salt, divided
- 1 lb *masa* (fresh or prepared from mix, page 24)
- ¼ cup lard

**For the *recado negro*:**
- 4 each dried *ancho, mulato, gua- jillo* peppers, toasted nearly black, stemmed, seeded, recon- stituted
- ¼ cup *achiote* paste
- 2 – 3 tbsp apple cider vinegar
- 2 corn *tortillas*, charred
- 8 whole allspice berries
- 1 cinnamon stick
- 2 tsp whole black peppercorns
- 6 whole cloves
- 20 garlic cloves, peeled, roasted
- 1 medium white onion, roasted,
- 2 tbsp dried Mexican oregano, toasted
- 4 fresh *epazote* leaves
- 1½ tsp kosher salt
- 5½ cups chicken stock, divided
- 4 tbsp *masa harina*

**To assemble:**
- 1 tbsp corn oil
- 2 tbsp lard
- ½ cup *refritos* (page 132)
- 8 whole *habaneros* for garnish

**For the duck and *salbutes* (make ahead up to 1 day):** Preheat oven to 375°F. Cut duck into eight pieces, place in roasting pan. Sprinkle 3 teaspoons salt evenly throughout pieces, cover with aluminum foil. Roast until fork tender, about 1 hour. Debone and shred duck meat. Cover and store in refrigerator.

Place *masa* on a clean surface and create a well in the center. Place remaining salt and lard in well, and knead into *masa*. Divide into eight equal balls; cover with a moistened kitchen towel while working. Flatten each *masa* ball into a thick *tortilla*, about 4 ½ inches in diameter and ¼ inch thick. Store in refrigerator, directions on page 21.

**For the *recado negro*:** Place peppers in blender with *achiote* paste, vinegar, *tortillas*, allspice berries, cinnamon stick, peppercorns and cloves and purée 30 seconds. Add garlic, onion, oregano, *epazote* leaves and salt and purée into a smooth paste. Transfer paste to stock pot, add 5 cups chicken stock. Bring to a boil over medium heat, stirring constantly, 6 to 8 minutes. Reduce heat, add duck meat. Simmer for 30 minutes, stir occasionally. Combine remaining chicken stock with *masa harina* in a cup. Add to duck stew and cook until mixture thickens, about 10 minutes. Keep warm over low heat.

**To assemble:** Place *comal* over low heat, preheat 5 minutes. Drizzle corn oil over hot *comal* and wipe off excess with a paper towel. Melt 1 tablespoon lard on hot *comal*, cook *salbutes* 4 minutes per side. Transfer to platter. Spread *refritos* onto each *salbute*, and top with duck stew. Garnish and serve.

# Flautas
## Rolled Tacos Filled *with* Chicken | *Makes 4 servings*

*Flautas* are crunchy rolled *tacos* filled primarily with chicken. The great thing about them is that you can increase the length by overlapping the *tortillas* before rolling them up so they resemble their namesake, the musical flute or *flauta*. The secret to a good *flauta* is to achieve the right level of crispiness. Fry only a couple at a time to maintain a constant oil temperature: too low an oil temperature results in soggy *flautas*. For this recipe, a store-bought roasted chicken and corn *tortillas* can provide convenient alternatives.

2   tbsp olive oil
½   large white onion, sliced
1   *poblano* pepper, roasted, peeled, seeded, cut into strips
1   roasted chicken (3½ lb), bone-out, shredded (about 4 to 5 cups)
1   cup corn oil for frying
24  thin corn *tortillas* (page 74)

24  toothpicks to keep *tortillas* closed
4   Romaine lettuce leaves, shredded
1   cup *salsa de aguacate* (page 125)
¼   cup *crema Mexicana*
¼   cup *queso fresco*, crumbled

Place sauté pan over medium heat, add olive oil to pan and preheat 1 minute. Add onion. Cook 3 to 5 minutes until translucent and light brown, stirring occasionally. Add *poblano* strips and cook 1 minute. Add chicken and reduce heat to low. Cook chicken mixture over low heat for 4 minutes to evaporate liquid. Remove from heat.

Place cast iron skillet over medium heat, add corn oil to skillet and preheat to bubbling, about 3 to 4 minutes. Using a pair of tongs, dip *tortillas* in the hot oil to soften them. Transfer to a bowl. Place two softened *tortillas*, just overlapping, on a cutting board. Place about 2 tablespoons of shredded chicken spread out along the center of the overlapped *tortillas*. Tightly roll the *tortillas* around the chicken filling and secure with toothpicks. Repeat with remaining *tortillas* and chicken.

Working in batches, carefully drop the *flautas* into the hot oil and fry until crispy, about 3 minutes, turning the *flautas* once. Transfer them onto a sheet pan lined with paper towels.

Serve two *flautas* per plate, garnish together with ¼ cup of shredded lettuce, 2 tablespoons *salsa de aguacate*, a drizzle of *crema* and sprinkle 1 tablespoon *queso fresco*.

# Gorditas de tuétano
## Masa Cakes Stuffed *with* Braised Beef Shank *and* Marrow
### *Makes 4-6 servings*

Cooked bone marrow is a delicacy in Mexico but can be tricky to authentically recreate. I bought the entire beef shank with the bone, braised it and removed the marrow and shredded the meat. The long, slow cooking process produced a delicious result.

**For the filling:**

- 1½ cups tomato juice
- ½ cup fresh orange juice
- 2 tbsp fresh lime juice
- 2 tbsp *salsa inglesa* (Worcestershire sauce)
- 1 tsp kosher salt, divided
- 2 tsp ground black pepper, divided
- 2 garlic cloves, peeled
- 1 whole *serrano* pepper, stemmed
- 4 beef shanks (¾ lb each), bone-in, patted dry
- 2 tbsp corn oil
- 2 beers (about 3 cups liquid)

**To assemble:**

- 1 lb *masa* (fresh or prepared from mix, page 24)
- 1 tbsp corn oil

**For the filling (make ahead up to 2 days):** Preheat oven to 325°F. For marinade, pour tomato juice, orange and lime juices and *salsa inglesa* into blender. Add ½ teaspoon salt, 1½ teaspoons black pepper, garlic and pepper and purée until smooth. Set aside. Season the beef shanks with remaining salt and black pepper.

Place Dutch oven or oven-proof pot over medium heat, add corn oil to pot and preheat 2 minutes. Working two at a time, sear each beef shank, 2 minutes per side. Place seared shanks in pot and pour in marinade and beer, making sure liquid covers shanks ¾ of the way. Cover and place in oven. Braise until meat falls off bone, about 2 ½ to 3 hours. Remove from heat and allow to cool slightly. Scoop out cooked bone marrow and shred meat; place together in a bowl. Discard bones and reserve 1 cup of the liquid. To store, tightly wrap the meat and bone marrow and refrigerate.

**For the *gorditas* (make ahead up to 1 day):** Divide the *masa* into 12 equal balls; cover with a moistened kitchen towel while working. Using the palm of your hand, flatten each *masa* ball into a patty, about 4 inches in diameter and ½ inch thick. Store according to page 21 until ready to cook and assemble.

**To assemble:** Reheat meat, marrow and reserved liquid in a medium pan over medium heat and simmer for 10 minutes. Place *comal* over low heat, preheat 5 minutes. Drizzle with corn oil and wipe off excess with a paper towel. Working three at a time, place each patty on the hot *comal* and allow to fully cook, 3 minutes per side. Using a sharp knife, make a slit on one of the edges, forming a pouch. Fill each with equal amounts of meat. Transfer to a warm platter and serve.

# Garnachas de tinga de conejo
## Sweet Potato Masa Cakes *with* Rabbit Stew | *Makes 4 servings*

*Tinga* is a typical Mexican topping native to the state of Puebla that is comprised of finely shredded ground pork, beef or chicken and stewed in a mild tomato-chipotle pepper sauce. I decided to offer a twist and use rabbit here — the way my mother prepared it for my family at home. One of my favorite ways to eat *tinga* is as a topping on either *garnachas*, which are the delicious thick crispy potato-*masa* cakes offered in this recipe, or on *tostadas*, as described in the recipe's chicken variation on the following page. Top either with your choice of meat.

### For the *tinga*:

| | |
|---|---|
| 1 | whole rabbit (2 lb), skinned |
| 11 | garlic cloves, peeled, divided |
| 9 | dried bay leaves, divided |
| 1 | celery stalk, rough chopped |
| 1¼ | small onions, quartered, finely chopped, divided |
| 1 | medium carrot, peeled, coarsely chopped |
| 2 | tbsp plus ¾ tsp kosher salt, divided |
| 4 | tomatoes, roasted |

| | |
|---|---|
| 2 | canned chipotle peppers in adobo plus 4 tsp of sauce |
| 2½ | tsp whole cumin seeds |
| 1½ | tsp whole black peppercorns |
| 4 | whole cloves |
| 2 | tbsp lard |
| 1¼ | tsp dried Mexican oregano, crumbled |
| ¾ | tsp ground black pepper |
| ½ | cup cubed (½-inch) yellow potato, cooked al dente |

### For the *garnachas*:

| | |
|---|---|
| ¾ | lb sweet potato, washed |
| ½ | lb *masa* (fresh or prepared from mix, page 24) |
| 1 | cup corn oil |

| | |
|---|---|
| ½ | cup *queso fresco* for garnish |
| 4 | thinly sliced radishes for garnish |
| ½ | small carrot, peeled, cut into thin strips for garnish |

**For the *tinga* (make ahead up to 2 days):** Place rabbit in large stock pot with enough water to cover. Add 5 garlic cloves, 5 bay leaves, celery, onion, carrot and 2 tablespoons salt. Cook over high heat until boiling, lower heat and leave gently bubbling until tender, about 1 hour and 30 minutes. Remove from heat and allow to cool in liquid. Strain and reserve liquid for later use. Debone rabbit meat and finely shred. Set meat aside.

Place tomatoes, chipotle peppers and reserve liquid sauce, whole cumin seeds, black peppercorns, whole cloves, remaining bay leaves and garlic in blender and purée until to smooth. Set aside.

*(continued on page 50)*

Place cast iron skillet over medium heat, add lard to skillet and preheat 2 minutes. Add remaining onion and cook until translucent, about 3 minutes. Add purée and cook 4 minutes, stirring occasionally. Add meat and cook 2 minutes. Stir in oregano, remaining salt and black pepper and cook for 1 minute more. Carefully fold in potato. Transfer *tinga* to a bowl. Refrigerate tightly covered with plastic wrap.

**For the *garnachas* (make ahead up to 1 day):** Place sweet potato in a saucepan with enough water to cover. Bring to a boil and continue boiling until tender, about 40 minutes. Strain. Allow potato to cool, then peel and chop into large chunks. Set aside.

Place *masa* in a bowl. Slowly knead sweet potato into the *masa*. Knead gently to leave a chunky texture. Divide *masa* into eight equal balls; cover with a moistened kitchen towel while working. Using the palm of your hand, flatten each *masa* ball into an oval shape. Pinch a border ½ inch deep, working from the center to the edge. Flatten the bottom and make sure border is even throughout each *garnacha*. Place formed *garnachas* on a parchment-lined sheet pan, cover with the moistened towel while working. Wrap tightly with plastic wrap and refrigerate until ready to assemble.

**To assemble:** Place *tinga* in a pan with ½ cup of the reserved liquid. Simmer for 10 minutes. Place cast iron skillet over medium heat, add corn oil to skillet and preheat until bubbling, about 3 to 4 minutes. Working two at time, place each *garnacha* well-side down and cook until crispy, 2 minutes. Flip and cook 2 minutes to crisp bottom. Place cooked *garnachas* on paper towels to drain. Fill each *garnacha* with a generous ¼ cup of *tinga*. Garnish and serve.

...........................................................................................................

**Variation: *Tostadas de tinga de pollo*** (Crispy Tortillas Topped with Chicken Stew) Substitute rabbit with a 3 ½-pound whole chicken, cut into sections. Boil for 45 minutes to 1 hour, strain, debone and shred meat. Use half the amount of chicken for this recipe (good combination of both white and dark meat) and store the rest in an airtight container for later use. Follow the rest of the cooking directions as specified above.

Substitute the *garnacha* ingredients for 8 store-bought *tortillas*, ½ cup corn oil, ½ cup *refritos* (page 132), ¼ cup crumbled *queso fresco*, 2 thinly sliced radishes, 8 cilantro sprigs and ¼ thinly sliced red onion for garnishes. Place cast iron skillet over medium heat, add corn oil to skillet and preheat until bubbling, about 3 to 4 minutes. Using a fork, prick holes in *tortillas* to prevent them from inflating in the hot oil. Working one at a time, place each *tortilla* in hot oil and fry until crispy, 2 minutes per side. Place *tostadas* on paper towels to drain. Spread 2 tablespoons *refritos* on each *tostada*, divide reheated *tinga* evenly among *tostadas*. Garnish and serve.

# Tlayudas de carne asada
## Crispy Large Quesadillas *with* Beans, Cheese *and* Steak | *Makes 4 servings*

*Tlayudas* are large *quesadillas* of at least 16 inches in diameter and are usually cooked directly on the coals or on a grill. As I recreated these *antojitos*, I had the luxury of using the large griddle in my restaurant, which allowed me to make the *tlayudas* as large as possible. However, this recipe can be modified to fit your household cast iron skillet or *comal* by making the *tlayudas* smaller. I recommend finishing this recipe using an outdoor grill to emulate how it is done in the market food stands in Oaxaca, pictured here. It can be done indoors using a stove-top grill pan but it won't have the same smoky flavor of the authentic recipe.

**To marinate meat:**
- ¾ lb skirt steak
- 2 cups *salsa de ajo* (page 120)
- 1 canned chipotle pepper in adobo
- ½ cup olive oil
- ¼ tsp Maggi® *jugo sazonador*
- ½ tsp kosher salt

**For the *tlayudas*:**
- 1 lb *masa* (fresh or prepared from mix, page 24)
- 2 tsp lard, melted
- ¼ cup *refritos* (page 132)
- 4 cups grated Chihuahua cheese
- 1 avocado, peeled, pitted, sliced
- ½ cup *crema Mexicana*

**To marinate meat (make ahead up to 1 day):** Place skirt steak in a plastic food-storage bag. Place *salsa de ajo*, chipotle pepper, olive oil, Maggi® *jugo sazonador* and salt in blender and purée until smooth. Pour marinade into plastic bag. Secure bag and make sure marinade covers meat completely. Place bag in a pan and refrigerate. Allow meat to marinate for at least 1 hour or up to 1 day ahead.

**For the *tlayudas*:** Cut out 2 circles, about 16 inches in diameter, from a plastic grocery bag (page 74). Set aside. Divide the *masa* into four equal balls (or more, if making smaller *tlayudas*); cover with a moistened kitchen towel while working. Place *comal* (large enough to cook a 14-inch diameter *tortilla*) over low heat and preheat.

Place one dough ball between the plastic circles. Using the palm of your hand, flatten each ball, pressing down and rotating plastic circles with the other hand to keep even thickness, until you aquire a *tortilla* of about 14 inches in diameter.

Take the *tortilla* with the plastic circle still on it and flip onto the hot *comal*. Peel off the plastic. The heat from the *comal* might touch the plastic and cause it to shrink. If this happens, discard and use another plastic circle. Fully cook *tortilla*, about 2 minutes per side. Place a piece of parchment paper in between each cooked *tortilla* to prevent sticking.

*(continued on page 54)*

*(Tlayudos de carne asada* continued)

Prepare an outdoor grill or grill pan.

Transfer the steak to a sheet pan and discard marinade. Place steak on grill and cook the meat to medium-rare, about 3 to 4 minutes per side. Remove from grill, cover with aluminum foil and allow to rest for 15 minutes. Slice into strips.

Working one at a time, drizzle ½ teaspoon melted lard on one side of each *tortilla*. Spread 1 tablespoon *refritos* and sprinkle 1 cup cheese around *tortilla;* place on top about 8 slices (3 oz) of skirt steak, 4 avocado slices, and drizzle about 1 teaspoon *crema*. Close each *tortilla* to resemble a *quesadilla*, place on the grill and cook 3 minutes per side. Place each *tlayuda* on a large plate and serve. Accompany with an *agua fresca*.

**Variation: *Tlayudas con flor de calabaza*** (Crispy Large Quesadillas with Squash Blossoms) Substitute the filling ingredient with 24 raw squash blossoms, plus ½ cup cubed blanched *calabacita*, 1 cup roasted corn, ½ cup cooked chopped *nopales*, ½ cup chopped *epazote*, ¼ cup chopped white onion, 2 tablespoons olive oil.

In medium sauté pan, heat olive oil. Sauté white onion until translucent, about 3 minutes. Add *calabacitas* and cook until tender, about 5 minutes. Add *nopales* and corn kernels and cook for 3 more minutes. Finally, add the *epazote* and cook 1 minute more. Use 6 squash blossoms for each *tlayuda*. Follow the rest of the cooking directions as specified for *Tlayuda de Carne Asada*.

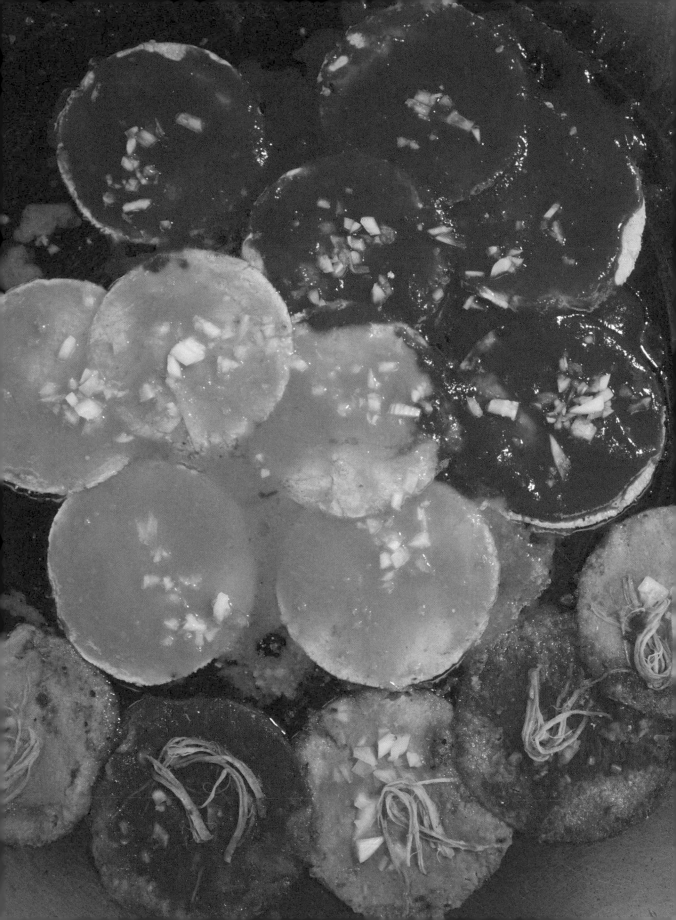

# Chalupitas
## Tortillitas Drenched *in* Salsa | *Makes 4 servings*

In a recent trip to Puebla, my brother and I visited Doña Lupita's street stand, located in a park near *avenida 21 oriente*. Doña Lupita sells delicious *chalupitas* that are drenched in red and green *salsas*, drizzled with lard and panfried on a large *comal*. Different sized corn *tortillas* are hard to find, so I recommend making your own small *tortillas* (page 74) for this recipe or I have offered an alternative using store-bought *tortillas* in the method below.

| | |
|---|---|
| 24 white corn *tortillas* (page 74) | ¼ cup *queso fresco*, crumbled, |
| ⅓ cup lard | optional |
| 1 cup *salsa de tomatillo* (page 119) | ¼ cup finely chopped white onion |
| 1 cup *salsa de ajo* (page 120) | for garnish |

Place the corn *tortillas* on a cutting board. Cut out a 3-inch circle from each *tortilla* using a cookie cutter. Set aside.

Place two medium-sized frying pans over medium heat, add 1 tablespoon lard to each pan and melt completely, preheat 2 minutes. Set the heat on low for each. Carefully pour the *salsa de tomatillo* in one pan and *salsa de ajo* in the other and stir. Bring both *salsas* up to a simmer, stir occasionally. Lower heat on each to keep warm.

Place cast iron skillet over medium heat, add ½ tablespoon lard to skillet and melt completely, preheat 2 minutes. Working three at a time, dip each of 12 small *tortillas* in *salsa de tomatillo*, place in pan with lard and panfry 1 minute per side. Transfer to serving plate. Wipe skillet with a paper towel and repeat process with remaining *tortillas* and the *salsa de ajo*. Garnish each with cheese, if using, and onions. Serve.

# Quesadillas fritas de mero
## Fried Rolled Tortillas Stuffed *with* Grouper Chunks | *Makes 6 servings*

Although the name of this *antojito* suggests that it is prepared in some way with cheese, a *quesadilla* doesn't necessarily have to contain *queso* or cheese. Throughout food stands in the streets of Mexico City, a *quesadilla* can have *chicharrón*, chicken or fish. However, as you travel to other parts of Mexico, a *quesadilla* usually means a half-moon shaped *tortilla* with melted cheese inside, along with other accompaniments. Debates arise as people think that these should be called *tacos* since calling them *quesadillas* can be misleading. In this recipe, I use the Mexico City definition of *quesadilla*. Regardless of the name, they are extremely delicious.

- 1 lb *masa* (fresh or prepared from mix, page 24)
- 1 lb fresh grouper, cut into 2-inch chunks
- 2 *chilaca* or *poblano* peppers, roasted, peeled, seeded, deveined, cut into strips
- 2 tomatoes, seeded, cut into strips
- 1 small white onion, thinly sliced
- 1½ tsp kosher salt
- Toothpicks as needed
- ¼ cup corn oil

Place *comal* over low heat, preheat 5 minutes. Divide the *masa* into six equal balls; cover with a moistened kitchen towel while working. Working one at a time, roll each *masa* ball into a cylinder and place in between two large pieces of parchment paper. Using the palm of your hand, lightly press down each cylinder to create an oval-shaped *tortilla*, about 10½ inches long and ¼ inch thick. Turn the *tortillas* as you flatten to ensure even thickness. Place *tortilla* on the hot *comal* and allow it to fully cook, about 2 minutes per side. Remove from heat and place on a sheet pan. Place a piece of parchment paper in between each *tortilla* to prevent them from sticking together.

Place 3 or 4 chunks of grouper in the center of each oval *tortilla*, 3 to 4 strips of pepper, 4 strips of tomato and 4 to 5 slices of white onion. Sprinkle ¼ teaspoon salt and close the *tortilla*. Secure at the edge with a toothpick so it won't open while it is frying.

Place cast iron skillet over medium heat, add corn oil to skillet and preheat 2 minutes. Lower heat to low-to-medium heat. Working two at a time, place each *quesadilla* in the hot oil and panfry until golden and crispy, about 8 to 10 minutes, flipping every 2 minutes to ensure even cooking and to fully cook the fish. Remove from heat and place on a sheet pan lined with paper towels. Place the sheet pan in oven to keep warm.

Remove the toothpicks before serving. Accompany with limes, *pico de gallo* and avocados, if desired.

# Quesadillas de flor de calabaza
## Squash Blossom Quesadillas | *Makes 4 servings*

As a young boy, my family and I moved to the outskirts of Puebla, out in the country, where we grew zucchini, beans, corn, tomatoes and watermelons and herded goats. I remember my mother sending me out to pick *flores de calabaza* from the emerging zucchini crop so she could make us *quesadillas*. Although those days in the country are long gone, I continue to use squash blossoms, raw or cooked, in salads, soups, *tacos* and *quesadillas*. They have a wonderful zucchini taste and can be purchased in specialty grocery stores or at the farmers market when in season.

⅓ cup olive oil
½ cup finely chopped white onion
24 *flores de calabaza* (squash blossoms), washed, stemmed
24 *epazote* sprigs, leaves only
1 tsp kosher salt

8 warm regular corn *tortillas* (page 74)
½ lb *quesillo* also known as queso Oaxaca
½ cup *salsa de tomatillo* (page 119)

Place sauté pan over medium heat, add ¼ cup olive oil and preheat 1 minute. Add onion and sauté until translucent, about 3 minutes. Add squash blossoms, *epazote* leaves and salt. Cook for 1 minute. Stir gently. The squash blossoms will wilt quickly. Immediately transfer the sautéed squash blossom mix to a bowl as it will continue to cook if left in the hot pan. Set aside.

Place *comal* over low heat, preheat 5 minutes. Place *tortillas* on the hot *comal*. In the center of each *tortilla* put 8 strings of *quesillo* and 3 cooked squash blossoms. Close *tortillas* into half-moon shape. Drizzle half the amount of remaining olive oil on one side of the *quesadillas*. Flip them and allow them to crisp up, about 2 minutes. While they are cooking, drizzle the remaining olive oil on the other side. Flip the *quesadillas* and allow them to crisp on the other side, about 2 minutes. Transfer to warm plates and serve.

Open each *quesadilla* just before eating and drizzle in 1 tablespoon *salsa de tomatillo*.

....................................................................................................

**Variation: *Quesadillas de huitlacoche*** (Mexican Corn Truffle Quesadillas) Substitute filling ingredients with ¼ cup olive oil, ½ small white onion, thinly sliced, 1 (8 oz) can *huitlacoche* (page 247), 2 *chilaca* or *poblano* peppers, roasted, peeled, deveined, cut into strips, 2 tablespoons chopped *epazote*, ½ teaspoon kosher salt, 8 regular warm corn *tortillas* (page 74) and 2 ⅔ cups grated Chihuahua cheese.

Place sauté pan over medium heat, add 2 tablespoons olive oil to pan and preheat 1 minute. Add onion and cook until translucent, about 3 to 5 minutes. Add *huitlacoche*, peppers and *epazote*. Reduce heat and cook 4 minutes. Add salt. Remove from heat. Follow the rest of the cooking directions as specified above. Omit *salsa de tomatillo*.

## Sopes
### Crunchy Potato Masa Bowls | *Makes 6 servings*

This is a very versatile *masa* recipe that gives a nice crunchy result. It is a combination of *masa* and cooked potatoes, which provides the crunchy element. This *masa* can be shaped into normal-sized *sopes* — deep-ridge *masa* bowls (about 2 inches in diameter) popular in Jalisco — or small bite-sized *sopesitos*, (about ½ inch in diameter) perfect for parties. The photo opposite shows these *sopesitos* topped with *carnitas* (pork variation) of my recipe for *taquitos de cachete* (page 105). Enjoy either of these meats on this deliciously crunchy *sope*.

1 **large (10 oz) Idaho potato, peeled, coarsely chopped**
½ **lb *masa* (fresh or prepared from mix, page 24)**
½ **cup corn oil**

Place potato in a saucepan with enough water to cover. Bring to a boil and continue boiling until tender, about 20 minutes. Strain. Transfer cooked potato to a sheet pan and place in refrigerator to cool down completely, about 1 hour.

Place *masa* in a bowl. Slowly knead potato into the *masa*. Knead gently as not to mash the potato too much to leave a chunky texture. Divide the *masa* mixture into six equal balls; cover with a moistened towel while working. Using the palm of your hand, flatten each *masa* ball into a patty, about 2 ¼ inches in diameter. Pinch a border ½ inch deep throughout the circumference. Flatten the base.

Place cast iron skillet over medium heat, add corn oil to skillet and preheat until bubbling, about 3 to 4 minutes. Working one at a time, place each *sope* well-side down and allow it to panfry for 3 minutes. Flip and spoon hot oil into the bowl to help cook the center. Remove from oil and place on a sheet pan lined with paper towels.

Top with *carnitas* (page 105) or try beef cheeks from *taquitos de cachete* (page 105). Garnish with crumbled cheese, onions and sliced *jalapeño* peppers.

# Elotes asados
## Roasted Corn Cobs *on a* Stick | *Makes 4 servings*

A common street food and one of the simplest and most delicious corn-based snacks is the *elote asado* or *en vaso*. It is corn grilled in its husks, spread with butter or mayonnaise, sprinkled with *queso Cotija*, chili powder and a few drops of lime juice. The same ingredients are also served off the cob and layered in a plastic cup. These two items are usually sold from the same *puesto*, or stall. Instead of butter or mayonnaise, I use *crema Mexicana* for a tangier taste. This recipe is best done on an outside grill, but you can recreate it indoors with the help of a cast iron skillet.

- 2 dried *guajillo* peppers, stemmed, toasted
- 1 dried *chile de árbol* pepper, stemmed, toasted
- 1 tsp paprika
- ½ tsp table salt
- 4 ears of corn with husks
- 4 long wood skewers
- 2 Persian limes
- ¼ cup *crema Mexicana* or mayonnaise
- ½ cup *queso Cotija*, crumbled

Place dried peppers in blender or spice grinder and process until a powder is achieved. Transfer to a bowl and add paprika and table salt. Mix to combine. Set aside.

Place cast iron skillet over medium to high heat, preheat 5 minutes or prepare an outdoor grill. Place corn and roast for 10 minutes, turning every 2 minutes. Remove from heat and pull back the husks. Remove and discard the silk. Carefully insert the sharp end of the skewer into the end of the corn. Over each *elote asado*, squeeze half a lime, spread 1 tablespoon *crema*, sprinkle 2 teaspoons cheese and finish with a pinch to ¼ teaspoon of the chili mixture.

...........................................................................................................

**Variation:** *Elotes en vaso* (Corn in a Cup) Place ears of corn still in husks in large stock pot with enough water to cover and 3 tablespoons kosher salt. Bring to a boil. Leave boiling until kernels are tender to the touch, about 30 minutes. Drain and cool slightly. Remove and discard the husks. Cut off point end of each ear with a sharp knife to make a stable base. Slowly run a sharp knife over the kernels of each ear to remove. Toss kernels in a bowl with about ⅛ teaspoon fresh lime juice. Garnish with ½ tablespoon chopped *epazote*. Serve in small cups with spice mixture and *crema* on the side.

# Chileatole

### Spicy Corn Porridge | *Makes 6 servings*

As kids, we used to buy *chileatole* — a bright green, hearty porridge — at the *elotes asados* and *esquites* stand during the cold, winter months. All corn based, *chileatole* is served warm or at room temperature. I wanted my interpretation to be spicy and flavorful; two things I believe are essential to combat the cold. Enjoy!

- ¼ lb *masa para tamales*
- 1 cup chopped white onion, divided
- 1 *jalapeño* pepper, seeded, deveined
- 1 *poblano* pepper, seeded, deveined
- 1 *serrano* pepper, seeded, deveined
- ¼ bunch cilantro, coarsely chopped
- 6 *epazote* sprigs, leaves only
- 3 *tomatillos*, husks removed, coarsely chopped
- 2 ears of corn, roasted
- 1 tbsp lard
- 1 tbsp kosher salt
- ¼ tsp fresh lime juice

Dissolve *masa para tamales* in 1 cup water and set aside. This will serve as the thickening agent for the *chileatole*.

Place ½ cup chopped onion, peppers, cilantro, *epazote*, *tomatillos* and ½ cup water in blender and purée into a smooth paste. This will be the coloring and flavoring agent. Set aside.

Using a sharp knife, remove corn kernels from the cobs and set aside. Place saucepan over medium to high heat, completely melt lard in pan and preheat 2 minutes. Add remaining chopped onion and cook until it translucent, about 3 minutes. Add the corn kernels and cook for 5 minutes, stirring constantly to prevent from sticking. Stir in the *masa*-water mixture plus 2 more cups water. Stir until boiling, about 5 minutes. Remove from heat and cool slightly. Add the green paste and salt to taste. Stir to combine.

Add a few drops of lime juice to each bowl just before serving.

# Esquites

### Corn *in a* Cup Flavored *with* Epazote | *Makes 6 servings*

*Esquites* is a Mexican *antojito* usually sold in the same food stalls or carts as *elotes*. *Esquites* are different from your typical corn in a cup as the corn must be extremely fresh and young. It is harder to find here in the United States but ask the produce clerk at a Mexican grocery store for this information, or look for it in your local farmers market when corn is early in its season. To be able to recreate the authentic street flavor of this dish, I use extremely young white corn only and a good-quality chicken stock.

½ cup olive oil
1 cup finely chopped white onion
4 garlic cloves, peeled, minced
12 ears of white corn, kernels only
2 whole *serrano* peppers, stemmed, minced

6 cups chicken stock
¼ cup chopped *epazote*
2 tsp dried Mexican oregano, crumbled
2 tsp kosher salt
6 lime slices for garnish

Place cast iron skillet over medium heat, add olive oil to skillet and preheat 2 minutes. Add onion and garlic and sauté for 3 minutes. Add corn kernels and cook for 2 minutes. Add peppers and sauté for 2 minutes more.

Slowly add chicken stock and bring to a boil, about 2 minutes, while stirring occasionally. Stir in *epazote* and oregano. Reduce heat to low and simmer until the liquid has reduced by half the amount, about 8 minutes. Add salt.

Serve in plastic cups, about ¾ cup each per serving. Garnish and accompany with mayonnaise and chili powder if desired.

Tacos

**Tacos** — soft corn *tortillas* filled with different meats, vegetables and even stews — are some of the most popular items in the street food scene. *Taco* fillings can be categorized in two ways: *a la plancha* or *de cazuela*, from the griddle or in a pot. A typical appliance in *taco* stands throughout Mexico is a large *plancha* or griddle, on one side they warm the *tortillas* for the *tacos*, and on the other side, cook the fillings. This cooking method produces a wonderful sear to the outside of meats and a crispiness to vegetables. The seasoned griddle infuses additional flavor into the filling ingredients as they cook. Other *taco* stands, alternatively, have a table set up with many *cazuelas* — earthenware pots — filled with *guisados*, or stews. When ordering, you tell the vendor what type of *taco* you would like based on the selection of fillings in the *cazuelas*, such as *guisado de chicharrón* or *chile verde* among many others. The *cazuela* is the epitome of *comida casera*, or the home-cooked meal. The cooking of a stew in a Mexican home kitchen is an ode to the principles of "slow food" — made with local, artisanal ingredients and cooked with love, in some cases, for many hours. Regardless of the style of filling, however, a *taco* is not a *taco* without handmade *tortillas*.

Two types of *tacos* are served from the street vendors: *tacos* and *taquitos*, which are distinguished by the size of the *tortilla* (page 74). I have found that by adding *refritos* (page 132), *frijoles de olla* (page 132) and *arroz a la Mexicana* or *blanco* (page 133) to many of these *taco* recipes they become more satisfying as well as flavorful. Keep in mind these are optional items. If you have them readily available in your refrigerator, as it is the common practice in Mexican homes (page 16), you can more easily replicate the street food flavor experience.

The recipes found in this chapter offer my interpretation of the delicious *tacos* I grew up eating or have encountered in my many visits to Mexico. They hold a special place in my heart. The faces of the customers and vendors I have encountered along the way are pictured on the following two pages. These are the people of Mexico who give the experience of eating in the streets a feeling of connection and a genuine flavor.

# Tortillas

Making *tortillas* is a deep-rooted tradition in Mexican culture. Growing up, I saw my grandmother leave at dawn with her *nixtamal* to the community mill and return with her bundle of fresh *masa* in hand ready to make *tortillas* outdoors. She set up a wood-burning fire and placed a piece of metal on top to act as a *comal*. There was nothing like her *tortillas*.

I highly recommend making fresh *tortillas* and using fresh *masa*, if possible (page 24). A *tortilla* press and *comal*, or cast iron griddle, will be necessary equipment. A *tortilla* press has a lever and comes in two basic sizes: 6 and 8 inches in diameter made of either cast iron or shiny aluminum. Before starting: preheat *comal* and line the inside of the *tortilla* press with plastic to help prevent the *masa* from sticking. Cut out two plastic circles about 7 to 8 inches in diameter from a clear plastic bag, such as those found in the produce section, or a zip-locking storage bag. Use and reuse these to line the inside of the press when making *tortillas*.

[ MASTER RECIPE ]

**Recipe for handmade *tortillas*:**
- 2  lb fresh *masa*
- 1  cup corn *masa* flour

Place fresh *masa* on a clean surface and adjust consistency by slowly adding *masa* flour and 1 cup water until achieving a soft, moist, smooth dough.

**Regular-size** (about 6 to 7 inches in diameter)
Evenly divide the *masa* into 18 balls. Place each ball in the *tortilla* press between two pre-cut plastic circles. Lightly press to form a $\frac{1}{16}$-inch-thick *tortilla*.

**For small-size** (about 4½ inches in diameter)
Divide *masa* into 42 balls.

Open press and remove the top plastic. Flip the bottom plastic onto the palm of your hand, raw *tortilla* side down. Peel off plastic and transfer raw *tortilla* to the hot *comal*. When the *tortilla* looks opaque, about 30 seconds, flip. Cook for 30 seconds more. Flip once again and as soon the *tortilla* puffs up, about 30 seconds, remove from heat. Wrap cooked *tortillas* in a dry, clean kitchen towel until ready to use. Store cooked *tortillas* in a sealed container or storage bag in the refrigerator for up to 1 week.

*Taquitos* require the small *tortilla*, and are served five *taquitos* per order; while *tacos* call for regular-sized *tortillas*, and are served two to three per order. To accommodate large amounts of fillings overlap two regular-sized *tortillas* when assembling. Although the smaller *tortillas* help to emulate the feel of street *taquitos*, regular *tortillas* can be used for these recipes and adjusted by adding more filling to each of the *tacos*.

**Warming Pre-cooked Handmade or Store-bought *Tortillas*:** The recipes for this chapter call for "warm" *tortillas*. Just before serving, reheat the *tortillas* by placing them on a hot *comal* for 1 minute, flipping until completely warmed. Keep them warm wrapped in a dry, clean kitchen towel until ready to assemble *tacos*.

# Tacos de chile relleno
## Stuffed Poblano Pepper Tacos | *Makes 6 servings*

On our way to Puebla to look for artisanal items, we became extremely hungry and were still far from our destination. Thankfully, a young man riding a tricycle passed by selling *tacos de chile relleno*. They were delicious. Here is our interpretation of that memorable experience.

**For *chiles rellenos*:**

- 6 large *poblano* peppers, roasted, peeled, stem intact
- 1 roasted chicken (3½ lb), bone-out, shredded, (about 4 to 5 cups)
- 1 recipe *salsa de jitomate y chile verde* (page 125) substitute *serrano* peppers in recipe with 4 dried bay leaves
- 1 cup grated Chihuahua cheese

**To assemble:**

- 6 eggs, separated
- 1 cup corn oil
- Flour for dusting
- ¾ cup *frijoles de olla* (page 132), optional
- ½ cup of *arroz a la Mexicana* (page 133), optional
- 12 regular-sized *tortillas* (page 74), warm

**For *chiles rellenos* (make ahead up to 1 day):** To prepare peppers: insert a sharp knife into each *poblano* pepper 1-inch from stem. Make sure the knife pierces the heart-shaped seed core. Push knife downward and core should pop off. Make a 2-inch-long incision starting from stem to create a small flap but keep the pepper intact for stuffing. Gently rinse each pepper to remove any remaining seeds.

Combine shredded chicken with *salsa de jitomate y chile verde* in a bowl and toss to combine. Add salt to taste. Working one at a time, take each *poblano* pepper and gently stuff it with 2 tablespoons cheese, followed by ¼ cup chicken. Repeat again to completely stuff *poblano*. Close the flap. With a damp, clean kitchen towel, wipe off excess sauce. Place stuffed peppers on a sheet pan lined with parchment paper, wrap with plastic and refrigerate until ready to use.

**To assemble:** Using a mixer fitted with whisk attachment, pour egg whites into bowl and whisk to medium stiff peaks. Lower speed and add each yolk one at a time.

Place cast iron skillet over medium heat, pour corn oil to skillet and preheat to bubbling, about 3 to 4 minutes. Working one at a time, lightly dust each *chile relleno* with flour and dip in the egg batter. Place in hot oil and fry until golden brown, about 3 to 4 minutes per side. Place cooked *chiles rellenos* on paper towels to drain. Place uncovered in a warm oven while you work.

Place two warm *tortillas* just overlapping each other. Sprinkle 2 tablespoons each *frijoles de olla* and *arroz a la Mexicana*, if using, in the center of each set of overlapped *tortillas*. Stack *chile relleno* in the center of the overlapping *tortillas* and close.

........................................................................................................

**Variation: *Taquitos de jalapeños rellenos*** (Stuffed Jalapeño Taquitos) Substitute *poblano* peppers with 12 to 18 *jalapeño* peppers and *tortillas* for 12 to 18 small-sized *tortillas*. Follow the rest of the directions as specified above.

# Tacos de nopal con bistec de puerco
## Pork Chop *with* Seared Cactus Paddle Tacos | *Makes 4 servings*

In the corner of *7 sur y 21 poniente* in Puebla, stands a young girl named Paola (pictured opposite) who has been keeping her mother's memory alive through food since 1985. She and her brother inherited the business from their mother, who initiated the *puesto* on that very corner many years ago. Paola honors her mother every day by making delicious *gorditas* and *tacos de nopal con bistec de puerco*. She uses only blue corn *tortillas* just as her mother did.

**To bread pork chops:**

- 4 **pork sirloin chops, pounded to ⅛-inch thick**
- ¾ **cup all-purpose flour**

- 2 **eggs, lightly beaten**
- ¾ **cup panko bread crumbs**

**To assemble:**

- ½ **cup corn oil**
- 4 *nopales* **(cactus paddles), cleaned (page 249)**
- 1 **cup** *salsa de aguacate* **(page 125)**
- ½ **lb** *quesillo* **also known as** *queso Oaxaca*

- 1 **avocado, peeled, pitted, sliced**
- 4 **regular-sized** *tortillas* **(page 74), warm**

**To bread pork chops:** Working one at a time, season each side of pork chops with salt and pepper. Pass each pork chop through the flour, beaten eggs and finally through the panko bread crumbs, shaking off excess each time. Place breaded pork chops on a sheet pan until ready to panfry.

Place cast iron skillet over medium heat, add corn oil to skillet and preheat to bubbling, about 3 to 4 minutes. Working one at a time, place each breaded pork chop in the hot oil and fry until golden brown, 3 minutes per side. Place cooked pork chops on paper towels to drain. Place in a warm oven until ready to assemble *tacos*.

**To assemble:** Preheat *comal* over low heat, 5 minutes. Working one at a time, place each *nopal* on the hot *comal* and sear, 6 minutes per side. Place on a cutting board. Using a pair of tongs, hold each seared cactus paddle and slice into strips ½ inch from the top. Keep in warm oven until ready to assemble *tacos*. Place each pork chop on warm *tortilla* and top in this order: *nopal*, ¼ cup *salsa de aguacate*, a handful of *quesillo* and 4 avocado slices.

.........................................................................................................

**Variation:** *Tacos de nopal y jamón* (Seared Cactus Paddle with Ham Tacos) Substitute pork chops with 2 pounds of a good-quality smoked or brined ham. Reduce amount of corn oil to ¼ cup and pan-fry each ham slice for 2 minutes per side. Slice 1 small onion and caramelize, about 10 minutes. Follow cooking directions as specified above. To make the *taco* a breakfast item, top each *taco* with a fried egg.

# Tacos "placeros" de carne adobada
## Adobo-Marinated Flank Steak Tacos | *Makes 4 servings*

*Tacos "placeros"* are so called because they are quick, easy and delicious *tacos* generally sold in the *plazas* or town squares. In a recent visit to Oaxaca, my brother Ruben and I saw these *tacos* near the *zócalo*. The nearby *mercado 20 de noviembre* by the streets of *Aldama, 20 de noviembre, Arteaga y Miguel Cabrera* — pictured on previous pages — offers a unique fresh, fast dining experience. Customers visit the many food stalls in the market to buy vegetables, meats and sides. They can then take them to one of several *puestos* with grills and griddles set up to cook these fresh *taco* ingredients on-site, to order. What a great concept!

**For marinade and steak:**

- 4 dried *guajillo* peppers, reconstituted
- 2 dried *ancho* peppers, reconstituted
- ¼ cup finely chopped white onion
- 2 garlic cloves, peeled
- ½ tsp whole cumin seeds
- 8 allspice berries
- 1 cinnamon stick
- 2 dried *hojas de aguacate*, optional
- 8 whole cloves
- 2 tomatoes, roasted
- 2 tsp chicken base, or bouillon cube
- 2 tbsp lard
- 3 lbs flank steak, butterflied, pounded to ⅛-inch thickness

**To assemble:**

- 12 *cebollitas cambray* (Mexican green onions)
- 12 regular-sized *tortillas* (page 74), warm

**For marinade (make ahead up to 3 days) and steak:** Place peppers in blender, along with onion, garlic, cumin, allspice berries, cinnamon stick, *hojas de aguacate*, if using, whole cloves, tomatoes and chicken base. Purée into a thick, smooth paste.

Place saucepan over medium heat, add lard to pan and completely melt, preheat 2 minutes. Add paste and reduce heat. Allow to simmer, 20 minutes, stirring occasionally. Remove from heat and allow to cool completely. Store in plastic air-tight container and refrigerate until ready to use.

Place the steak in a plastic food storage bag. Pour marinade into bag. Secure bag and make sure marinade covers steak completely. Place bag in a pan or container and refrigerate. Allow the meat to marinate for at least 3 hours or up to overnight.

**To assemble:** Prepare outdoor grill or grill pan.

Transfer steak to sheet pan and discard marinade. Place steak on the hot grill and cook to medium-rare, about 3 to 4 minutes per side. Cook onions on grill for 4 to 6 minutes, turning occasionally. Remove steak from grill, cover with aluminum foil and allow it to rest for 15 minutes. Slice into strips.

Arrange warm *tortillas* on warm plates. Place 3 to 4 steak strips (1.5 oz) in each *tortilla*. Serve with the grilled onions.

# Tacos de tránsito de lujo
**Luxury Pig's Feet Tacos** | *Makes 4 servings*

*Tacos de tránsito* are made of pig's feet panfried in an egg batter with a unique twist. The pig's feet are not deboned, which requires picking out the cartilage as you eat them. They are delicious and worth the trouble. Another option exists, however: *tacos de lujo* or "luxury" *tacos*, the recipe which I offer here. These *tacos* are a "luxury" since they are made with deboned pig's feet making them easier to eat but requiring a little more work for the cook. Pig's feet are available in local Mexican butcher shops or in the frozen pork meat section, packaged and quartered.

**For pig's feet:**
- 6 lbs pig's feet, packaged, quartered, washed
- 8 dried bay leaves
- 8 garlic cloves, peeled
- 4 tsp kosher salt
- 2 tsp dried Mexican oregano

**To assemble:**
- 9 eggs, separated
- ¾ cup all-purpose flour, divided
- 1½ cups corn oil for frying
- 8 regular-sized *tortillas* (page 74), warm
- ½ cup *refritos* (page 132), optional
- 1 cup *arroz blanco* (page 133), optional
- 1 whole red or green *jalapeño* pepper, stemmed, sliced into rounds for garnish

**For pig's feet (make ahead up to 1 day):** Place pig's feet in large stock pot with enough water to cover. Add bay leaves, garlic, salt and oregano. Cook over high heat until boiling, lower heat and leave gently bubbling until fork tender, about 3 hours. Remove from heat, strain and transfer cooked pig's feet to a sheet pan. Allow to cool slightly, about 20 minutes.

Working one by one, place each cooked pig's foot in the palm of your hand. Carefully remove bones one by one, keeping the shape as much as possible. Sprinkle 1 tablespoon flour on the meat and place it on a piece of plastic wrap. Wrap each into a tight cylinder shape. Place individually wrapped pig's feet on a sheet pan and refrigerate at least 1 hour or until ready to assemble.

**To assemble:** Using a mixer fitted with whisk attachment, pour egg whites into bowl and whisk to medium stiff peaks. Lower speed and add yolks one at a time. Unwrap pig's feet and set aside.

Place cast iron skillet over medium heat, add corn oil to skillet and preheat to bubbling, about 3 to 4 minutes. Working one at a time, lightly dust each cylinder with remaining flour and place in a bowl. Spoon the egg batter over the dusted cylinder and carefully fold together. Place in hot oil and fry until golden brown, about 3 to 4 minutes per side. Spoon hot oil on top while frying. Place cooked pig's feet on paper towels to drain. Place uncovered in a warm oven while you work.

Place two warm *tortillas* just overlapping each other, spread 2 tablespoons *refritos* and *arroz*, if using. Stack a pig's foot in the center of each set of warm *tortillas*. Garnish and serve. Accompany with *salsa de ajo* (page 120).

# Tacos Roger

The recipe developed for *tacos de tránsito de lujo* was inspired by a special *taco* served at *Tacos Roger*, a *taco* stand located in Puebla, in the *colonia la Paz* by *calle oriental y Atlacomulco* across the street from the *cuartel de policía*, or police headquarters. This zone or *colonia* is categorically known as "tránsito," a word referring to the police officers. When locals speak about Roger's well-renowned *tacos* they refer to them knowingly as *tacos de tránsito*.

Rogelio, or Roger *(pictured opposite)*, learned to cook from his grandmother. For 20 years now, Roger has operated his *taco* stand in the *zona de tránsito*. He and his family wake up at 5:00 a.m. every day to prepare all the food for the stand at home and put it in baskets to transport so that by 9:00 a.m. the stand will be ready to serve his customers.

People congregate outside and line up to order *tacos de milanesa*, *chipotle*, *poblano y chicharrón*, *pata*, *salpicón* and more. They either stand to eat these enormous *tacos* or sit at the plastic tables set outside. His stand has a tarp set up with additional seating and is open until 5:00 p.m.

Pig's feet *tacos* are my favorite here, and I decided to offer my gratitude to Rogelio, who is an example of the purity, passion and tradition that lies behind Mexican street food.

# Guisado de cazuela de puerco con chile verde
## Pork Stew *in a* Tomatillo Sauce | *Makes 4-8 servings*

The concept of *guisados* reinforces my opinion that Mexican street food is a model of "slow food" cooking. People think that the food is prepared casually in the streets but that's not the case. Vendors take hours to prepare these hearty stews at home then pack and transport them to their food stands at the local *tianguis* or markets. The *guisado de puerco con chile verde* is a common one found in such markets. It is both delicious and filling in a *taco*. In this recipe, along with the adjacent recipe (page 91), the cooking liquid of the stew meat is suitable to flavor other stews. Place in an airtight container or jar in the refrigerator. When ready to use, skim some of the fat and place in a small saucepan to heat up. For this particular recipe, the reserved liquid can be used also when making the *guisado de cazuela de chicharrón* (page 93).

**For stew meat:**

| | |
|---|---|
| 1½ lbs pork stew meat, cut in 2-inch chunks | 2 dried bay leaves |
| ½ large white onion, quartered | 2 garlic cloves, peeled |
| | 1½ tsp kosher salt |

**To assemble:**

| | |
|---|---|
| 6 medium *tomatillos*, husks removed, roasted | ¼ cup *pipicha* leaves, optional |
| ½ large white onion, roasted | ¼ small bunch cilantro, coarsely chopped |
| 2 garlic cloves, peeled, roasted | Pinch ground cumin |
| ½ whole *jalapeño* pepper, roasted, stemmed | 1 tsp kosher salt |
| 1 tbsp lard | 8 regular-sized *tortillas* (page 74), warm |

**For stew meat (make ahead up to 2 days):** Place stew meat in stock pot with enough water to cover. Add onion, bay leaves, garlic and salt. Cook over high heat until boiling, lower heat and leave gently bubbling until fork tender, about 1 hour. Strain and reserve at least 1 cup liquid. The rest can be stored as specified above. Cover meat and refrigerate until ready to assemble.

**To assemble:** Place *tomatillos*, onion, garlic, *jalapeño* and ½ cup reserved liquid in blender and purée into a smooth consistency. Place saucepan over medium heat, add lard to pan and completely melt, preheat 2 minutes. Add *tomatillo* sauce and bring to a boil. Add cooked stew meat plus ½ cup more reserved liquid and bring to a boil, lower heat and leave gently bubbling for 8 to 10 minutes, stir occasionally. Add *pipicha*, if using, cilantro, ground cumin and salt. Simmer and stir for 3 minutes more. Remove from heat.

Place ¼ cup *guisado* on each *tortilla*. Serve.

# Guisado de cazuela con carne a la Mexicana
## Beef Stew *with* Onion, Peppers *and* Tomato | *Makes 4-8 servings*

*Cazuelas* are great earthenware pots traditionally used in Mexican cooking. They bring back so many memories of my childhood. Due to the busy life in the kitchen, I rarely put out these pots — collected throughout the years from visits to Mexico — in fear that they might break. I wait for special occasions or our weekend brunch to display them for our customers. I highly recommend visiting artisanal ceramic shops when you are visiting Mexico as they have some beautiful treasures to buy.

**For stew meat:**
- 1½ lbs beef stew meat, cut in 2-inch chunks
- 1 small white onion, quartered
- 2 garlic cloves, peeled
- 1 dried bay leaf
- 1½ tsp kosher salt

**To assemble:**
- ¼ cup olive oil
- 1 small white onion, sliced
- 4 garlic cloves, peeled, minced
- ½ whole *jalapeño* pepper, stemmed, minced
- 4 tomatoes, cut into wedges
- ½ *poblano* pepper, roasted, peeled, deveined, seeded, cut into strips
- ½ tsp dried Mexican oregano
- Pinch ground cumin
- Pinch of ground cloves
- ½ small bunch cilantro, coarsely chopped, divided
- 8 regular-sized *tortillas* (page 74), warm
- ½ small white onion, finely chopped for garnish

**For stew meat (make ahead up to 2 days):** Place stew meat in medium stock pot with enough water to cover. Add onion, garlic, bay leaf and salt. Cook over high heat until boiling, lower heat and leave gently bubbling until fork tender, about 2 ½ hours. Strain and reserve at least ¼ cup liquid. Store remaining liquid in an airtight container in refrigerator.

**To assemble:** Place saucepan over medium heat, add olive oil to pan and preheat 2 minutes. Add cooked stew meat and allow it to brown, about 3 minutes. Add onion and cook until it is translucent, about 3 minutes. Add garlic and *jalapeño* and cook 2 minutes more. Lower heat; add tomatoes and *poblano* strips, cook until tomatoes release their juices, 3 minutes more. Add ¼ cup reserved liquid and bring to a boil, about 3 to 4 minutes. Lower heat and add oregano, cumin, ground cloves and half the amount of cilantro. Allow stew to simmer for 3 to 4 minutes more, stirring occasionally.

Place ¼ cup *guisado* on each *tortilla*. Garnish with remaining cilantro and onion and serve.

# Guisado de cazuela de chicharrón
### Softened Pork Skins Stew | *Makes 4-6 servings*

*Puestos de chicharrónes* are found throughout markets in Mexico City, where these crunchy pork skins are in containers under lamps, and customers can buy them by the kilo. In some stands, the large dried pork skin — usually the actual size of the pig it came from — is hanging from hooks, exposed in all its glory. *Chicharrónes* can be eaten dry, in a *tortilla* with *salsa de aguacate* (page 125) or cooked in a stew, as offered here. *Chicharrónes* wilt and reduce in size in hot liquid. They are available in the potato chips/snacks aisle in Mexican/Latin grocery stores. Keep in mind that *chicharrónes* are naturally very salty; therefore, add salt to taste.

| | |
|---|---|
| 10 medium *tomatillos*, husks removed, washed, roasted | 1 tsp dried Mexican oregano |
| 1 large white onion, quartered, roasted | ¼ tsp ground cumin |
| 6 garlic cloves, peeled, roasted | Pinch ground cloves |
| 1 whole *jalapeño* pepper, roasted, stemmed | ¼ cup *pipicha* leaves, optional |
| ¼ cup olive oil | 12 regular-sized *tortillas* (page 74), warm |
| 2 (4 oz) packages *chicharrónes* | ½ small bunch cilantro, coarsely chopped for garnish |
| 2½ cups beef stock (store-bought or reserved from recipe on page 90) | ½ small white onion, finely chopped for garnish |

Place *tomatillos*, onion, garlic and *jalapeño* in blender and purée into a smooth consistency.

Place saucepan over medium heat, add olive oil to pan and preheat 2 minutes. Add *tomatillo* sauce and bring up to a boil, 3 minutes, stirring continuously.

Add *chicharrónes*, stirring frequently to completely submerge them in sauce. Allow to wilt, about 3 minutes. Add beef stock or reserved liquid and bring to a boil. Reduce heat and leave gently bubbling for 5 minutes. Add oregano, cumin, cloves and *pipicha*, if using. Cook for 2 minutes more, stirring occasionally. Remove from heat.

Place ¼ cup stew on each *tortilla*. Garnish with cilantro and white onion.

# Tacos de papas, acelgas y champiñones
## Potatoes, Swiss Chard *and* Mushroom Tacos | *Makes 4-8 servings*

This vegetarian *taco* is fulfilling as well as hearty. This recipe shows that *tacos* are very versatile for any eating lifestyle. This vegetarian Mexican sauté can also be used as a substitute for the chicken in the *tacos de chile relleno* (page 77).

⅓ cup olive oil
½ medium white onion, sliced
6 garlic cloves, peeled, minced
½ lb white button mushrooms, cleaned, sliced or a mixture of your choice
½ large bunch Swiss chard, washed, stemmed
2 *chilaca* or *poblano* peppers, roasted, seeded, peeled, deveined, cut into strips

1 large yellow potato, roasted, cut into ½-inch cubes
1 tsp kosher salt
8 regular-sized *tortillas* (page 74), warm
1 recipe Hugo's *salsa Mexicana* (page 120), optional to accompany

Place cast iron skillet over medium heat, add olive oil to skillet and preheat 2 minutes. Add onion and cook until translucent, about 3 minutes. Add garlic and cook 2 minutes more.

Add mushrooms and cook until browned, about 5 minutes. Add Swiss chard and allow it to wilt, about 5 minutes. Add peppers and cook for 6 minutes. Add potato and continue to cook 2 minutes. Stir gently as not to mash the potato. Add salt.

Divide evenly among the *tortillas*. Serve with *salsa Mexicana*.

.......................................................................................

**Variation:** *Tacos de papa con chorizo* (Cubed Potato with Chorizo Tacos) Substitute filling with 1 tablespoon olive oil, ½ medium white onion, finely chopped, 6 garlic cloves, peeled, minced, 1 pound good-quality Mexican *chorizo*, and 2 large roasted yellow potatoes.

Place cast iron skillet over medium heat, add olive oil to pan and preheat 2 minutes. Add onion and cook for 3 minutes. Add garlic and cook 2 minutes more. Lower heat and add *chorizo*. Allow to fully cook, about 20 minutes. Add potatoes and cook for 5 minutes more, stirring occasionally. Add salt to taste. Follow the rest of the cooking directions as specified above. Omit *salsa*.

# Taquitos al pastor
## Slow-Roasted Pork Taquitos | *Makes 4-6 servings*

*Taquitos al pastor* are one of the most popular and common street *tacos*. The meat is sliced and pounded very thin, then arranged and roasted on a vertical spinning spit, or *trompo*. It is given this name because it resembles a spinning top, or *trompo* — a very popular Mexican toy. In some regions, such as in Mérida, a pineapple is skewered on top; in Puebla, an onion; and in other places, both. They slowly release their juices and continuously drip on the meat as it cooks. The vendor holds a parchment paper with a *tortilla* and slices off the meat, catching it in the *tortilla* to serve his customers. I have modified this recipe so that you can enjoy the taste of authentic *taquitos al pastor* at home.

**To marinate pork:**

- ½ cup *achiote* paste
- ¼ cup distilled white vinegar
- ¼ cup chicken stock
- ¼ cup orange juice
- 2 dried *guajillo* peppers, deveined, seeded, toasted, reconstituted
- 3 garlic cloves, peeled, roasted
- ½ tsp whole cumin seeds
- ½ tsp dried thyme leaves
- 2 dried bay leaves
- 2 dried *hojas de aguacate,* optional
- Small whole cinnamon stick, broken into pieces
- 1 tbsp kosher salt
- ½ tsp freshly ground black pepper
- 1 pork butt (4 lb), bone-in

**To assemble:**

- 2 fresh pineapple slices, cut into small slices
- ½ small white onion, thinly sliced
- Toothpicks as needed
- 12 small-sized *tortillas* (page 74), warm

**To marinate pork (make ahead up to 1 day):** Place *achiote* paste, vinegar, stock and orange juice in blender. Add peppers, garlic, cumin, thyme, bay leaves, *hojas de aguacate,* if using, and cinnamon stick pieces. Purée into a smooth paste.

Place pork butt on a clean cutting board. Sprinkle salt and black pepper evenly over entire pork butt. Transfer to plastic food storage bag. Pour in paste. Secure bag and make sure paste covers the pork butt completely. Place bag in pan or container and refrigerate. Allow meat to marinate at least 2 hours or up to overnight.

**To assemble:** Preheat oven to 375°F.

Transfer pork butt to a rack on a roasting pan. Pin pineapple and onion slices on top of pork butt with toothpicks. Cover and roast until fork tender, about 3 hours, basting with pan juices periodically.

Remove from oven, cover with aluminum foil and allow to rest for 15 minutes. Transfer to a clean cutting board and remove from bone. Remove pineapple and onion and discard toothpicks. Slice pineapple and onion separately and place each in bowls to use for garnish. Coarsely chop meat.

Place ¼ cup meat in each of the small *tortillas*. Top each with pineapple, onion and chopped cilantro, if desired.

# Taquitos dorados de papa
## Crispy Potato-Stuffed Taquitos | *Makes 4-8 servings*

These *taquitos* were inspired by the common, inexpensive and simple *tacos de papa* prepared in Mexican homes. I offered a twist by making the *tortillas* out of the *sopes* dough to produce a crunchier *taco*. I never imagined these *taquitos* would become such a popular item on my restaurant's menu. I hope you enjoy them as much as my customers.

**To make *taquitos*:**
- 1 recipe *sopes* dough (page 62), uncooked
- 2 medium yellow potatoes, cut into wedges
- 3 tbsp olive oil
- 3 garlic cloves, peeled, minced
- ¼ cup finely chopped white onion
- ½ tsp kosher salt

**To assemble:**
- ¼ cup corn oil
- 2 Napa cabbage leaves, washed, shredded
- 4 *chiles curtidos*, cut into strips (page 128)
- 1 cup *cebollas en vinagre* (page 128)
- 2 radishes, cut into thin strips for garnish
- 1 recipe *salsa de aguacate* (page 125), optional to accompany

**To make *taquitos* (make ahead up to 1 day):** Preheat oven to 400°F. Divide *sopes* dough into 16 equal dough balls, cover with plastic and refrigerate until ready to stuff. Place potato wedges in bowl. Add 1 tablespoon olive oil, garlic and half the amount of onion, toss to combine. Transfer coated potatoes to sheet pan, place in oven and roast until soft, 25 to 30 minutes. Remove from oven and transfer to a bowl. Mash into a purée.

Place cast iron skillet over medium heat, add remaining olive oil to skillet and preheat 2 minutes. Add remaining onion and cook until translucent, about 3 minutes. Lower heat and add mashed potatoes. Cook 2 minutes more, stirring continuously. Add salt. Remove from heat and allow to cool completely before stuffing *taquitos*.

Working one at a time, use a *tortilla* press to lightly press each dough ball into a small *tortilla*, about 4 ½ inches in diameter. Place 1 tablespoon mashed potato on the right half of each *tortilla*. Flip the other half over on top of mixture, enclosing filling. Remove from *tortilla* press and transfer to a parchment-lined sheet pan. Wrap in plastic and refrigerate until ready to pan-fry.

**To assemble:** Place cast iron skillet over medium heat, add corn oil to skillet and preheat to bubbling, 3 to 4 minutes. Working in batches of four, place each *taquito* in hot oil and pan-fry until golden brown, about 2 to 3 minutes per side. Using a slotted spatula, transfer cooked *taquitos* to paper towels to drain.

Fill each *taquito* with a pinch of shredded cabbage, 4 strips of *chiles curtidos*, 2 *cebollas en vinagre*. Garnish and serve. Accompany with *salsa de aguacate*.

# Taquitos de cachete

### Beef Cheek Confit Taquitos | *Makes 4 servings*

In Mexico, *taco* vendors slow roast one whole animal — most commonly, the pig — and sell *tacos* out of the different cuts of that animal, such as *taquitos de cachete* (cheek), *lengua* (tongue), *pancita* (stomach), *cabeza* (head) and *surtida* (a little bit of everything). My favorite *tacos* are those filled with pig cheeks. These are usually the first cut to sell out, which means customers arrive earlier the next day! In my interpretation of these popular *taquitos*, I used beef cheeks because they are more readily available from the butcher but just as delicious.

**To prepare beef cheeks:**

| | |
|---|---|
| 1 tsp whole cumin seeds | 2½ lbs beef cheeks, patted dry |
| 1 tsp dried thyme leaves | 2 lbs lard |
| 2 dried bay leaves | 1 cup beer |
| 2 dried *guajillo* peppers, stemmed | 2 tbsp fresh orange juice |
| 2 garlic cloves, peeled | 1 tbsp fresh lime juice |
| | 2 tbsp kosher salt |

**To assemble:**

| | |
|---|---|
| 20 small-sized *tortillas* (page 74), warm | 1½ cups finely chopped cilantro |
| 1½ cups finely chopped white onion | 8 *limones criollo* (key limes), quartered |
| | 1 recipe *salsa de habanero* (page 127), optional to accompany |

**To prepare beef cheeks (make ahead up to 2 days):** Place cumin, thyme, bay leaves, peppers, garlic and ½ cup water in blender and purée into a smooth consistency. Transfer to bowl. Rub on all sides of beef cheeks and set aside.

Preheat oven to 400°F. Place Dutch oven or oven-proof pot over medium heat, add ¼ cup lard to pot and completely melt, preheat 2 minutes. Sear each beef cheek, about 2 minutes per side. Place seared beef cheeks on a sheet pan and cover with aluminum foil. Add remaining lard to pot and melt completely. Carefully drop beef cheeks into melted lard, place in oven, covered. Cook 2 hours.

Add beer, orange juice and lime juice. Cover and return to oven until fork tender, about 40 minutes.

Dissolve salt in 1 cup water. Add to pot and return to oven for a final 20 minutes. Remove from the oven and set aside. Allow cheeks to cool in lard.

Once cool enough to handle, transfer cheeks from lard to a clean cutting board and chop.

**To assemble:** Divide meat among the small *tortillas*. Top each *taquito* with 1 tablespoon each onion and cilantro and place 2 lime quarters on each serving. Accompany with *salsa de habanero*.

................................................................

**Variation: *Taquitos de carnitas*** (Chopped Pork Shoulder Confit Taquitos) Substitute beef cheeks with 2 ½ pounds pork shoulder, quartered into large pieces. Follow the rest of the cooking directions as specified above.

# Taquitos de lengua
## Cow Tongue Taquitos | *Makes 4 servings*

Every time I eat these delicious *tacos* I remember my uncle Derio who owned both a *taco* stand and a used car dealership. These *tacos* were his favorite. I reminisce about one particular story when I was 15 years old and kept asking him to let me borrow one of his cars. The answer was always the same: "*No te lo puedo prestar mijo porque después chocas y luego ya no vamos a tener carro para traer los tacos,*" which roughly translates, "I can't let you borrow it, son, because you'll crash it, and we won't have a car to bring home the food for the *tacos.*" I hope you enjoy these *taquitos* as much as my uncle Derio. Cow tongue can be purchased at Mexican grocery stores in the frozen meats section or at the butcher counter. This recipe requires very little prep time but over four hours for steaming the meat in the pot. It is definitely worth the wait!

**For cow tongue:**

- 1 cow tongue (2¾ lbs), cleaned, ready to cook
- 2 tbsp kosher salt
- 2 banana leaves
- 25 small-sized *tortillas* (page 74), warm
- ½ large onion, finely chopped
- ½ small bunch cilantro, coarsely chopped

**To serve:**

1 recipe *salsa de jitomate y chile verde* (page 125) or *habanero* (page 127), optional to accompany

Preheat oven to 400°F.

Combine salt with about 6 cups water and pour into a roasting pan. Wrap cow tongue in banana leaves and place on a roasting rack, over the water. Place in oven, covered, and steam until fork tender, about 4 hours. Check water level every hour.

Remove from oven, wrapped, and allow to rest 15 minutes. Remove leaves and discard. Peel outer layer of cow tongue, discard, and chop the rest of the meat.

Divide meat among the small *tortillas*. Top each *taquito* with 1 tablespoon each onion and cilantro.

**To serve:** Accompany with *salsa de jitomate y chile verde* or *habanero*.

# Tacos de pescado
## Deep-Fried Fish Tacos | *Makes 4 servings*

Over the years, fish *tacos* have gained popularity outside of Mexico. This recipe is similar to those found in Baja California near the Mexican border. You will find these *tacos* served away from the coast as well in big urban areas like Mexico City. They are quick and delicious and their popularity is understandable. For this recipe, I use a light-colored beer for the batter to keep the beautiful white color of the fish. Remember to deep-fry just a couple of catfish strips at a time. Too many strips in the oil will lower the oil temperature causing the fish to soak up oil and turn soggy instead of crisp.

| | |
|---|---|
| 1 cup mayonnaise | 8 regular-sized *tortillas* (page 74), warm |
| 1 canned chipotle pepper in adobo plus 1 tsp of sauce | 2 Napa cabbage leaves, washed, shredded |
| 1½ cups all-purpose flour | ¾ cup *pico de gallo*, optional |
| 2 cups beer | 2 thinly sliced radishes for garnish |
| 10 to 12 cups corn oil for deep-frying | |
| ¾ lb catfish fillets, cut into strips | |

Place mayonnaise and chipotle pepper with sauce in blender and purée into a smooth consistency. Transfer to bowl or squeeze bottle and refrigerate until ready to use.

Place flour in bowl, pour in beer and whisk to a smooth consistency, making sure no lumps remain.

Pour corn oil into an electric fryer or in Dutch oven, preheat to 350°F.

Working two at a time, dip each catfish strip in the batter and place in hot oil. Deep-fry until golden brown, about 3 minutes. Place cooked fish on paper towels to drain.

Divide fried fish pieces among the *tortillas*. Top each *taco* with 2 tablespoons cabbage, drizzle about 2 teaspoons of chipotle mayo and finish with 2 tablespoons *pico de gallo*, if using. Garnish and serve.

Salsas

**Salsas** can be used in various ways, from marinades and sauces to stews, as well as being a simple topping for *tacos* or a dip for *totopos* — freshly made fried *tortilla* chips. When making a *salsa*, keep in mind that the recipes are not exact formulas with specific measurements and yields, since fresh tomatoes, peppers and onions vary in size and ripeness. Do use the cooking techniques, on page 116, to extract as much flavor as possible from these ingredients. It is the combination of such ingredients and how those flavors marry that create these delicious, sometimes spicy, and filling accompaniments.

Two types of *salsas* are featured here — fresh and cooked. Fresh *salsas* require little prep time and in most cases require just a few ingredients. I believe these recipes should be prepared right before serving, making just enough as needed. Once your first batch runs out, take a few minutes and prepare more. The more complex *salsas* — ones requiring cooking at some point in their preparation — can be made up to 3 to 4 days in advance. To store, cool *salsas* completely after making, transfer to a glass or plastic air-tight container. In this chapter, I include items such as *refritos*, *arroz a la Mexicana* or *cebolla en vinagre*. While they are not *salsas*, they play the role of a *salsa* by serving as an accompaniment, garnish or complement to many street food recipes in the book.

These *salsa* recipes can be adapted to your own palette. I offer a base amount of each ingredient but if a particular ingredient is your favorite and you would like to add more, I invite you to adjust the recipe. For example, I like the taste of garlic, thus I put several garlic cloves in all my recipes. You may reduce or increase the amount to fit your taste buds. Similar to the fresh peppers, more often than not, I use the whole fresh pepper with the seeds and veins. To reduce the heat level, remove seeds and veins from the peppers before using. Salt is another item that can be adjusted to your individual preference.

When using as a topping to an *antojito* or on *tacos*, *salsas* can be used interchangeably with each other. I offer my suggestions of which *salsa's* color, texture and flavor will best complement a dish, but don't be afraid to change things up by using your own favorites in place of my suggestions.

## Essential Techniques for *Salsa* Making

The following simple cooking methods help to emulate the delicious, flavorful and authentic Mexican *salsas*. Each of the steps below contributes an additional flavor dimension to the simple list of ingredients used in these recipes.

**Roasting** adds such a deep level of flavor that I like to roast the tomatoes, onions, garlic, *tomatillos* and fresh peppers in many of the recipes in this chapter as well as in other parts of the book. For the tomatoes, I use medium-sized plum tomatoes in all the recipes as these are the most suitable for roasting, dicing and puréeing due to their low water content. To roast, place tomatoes on a hot *comal* and roast 10 minutes, turning every 2 to 3 minutes to acquire an even roast and color.

Roast the rest of the items over an open fire using a pepper grill — available in gourmet kitchen supply stores — on a hot *comal* or under the broiler set on the highest setting. All these ingredients take about 8 to 10 minutes to roast in either method, turning ingredients every 3 to 4 minutes to acquire an even roast and color. To peel roasted fresh peppers: remove from heat, place in a bowl and cover with plastic wrap. Allow peppers to sweat for 15 minutes in order to loosen the charred skin. Peel under slowly running cold water. Discard the skin.

**Toasting and reconstituting** are important steps when preparing dried peppers to be used in a recipe. There is a huge spectrum of dried peppers used in Mexican cuisine — *guajillo*, *pasilla*, *ancho*, *chile de árbol* and more (see Glossary).

> **To toast:** Remove stem and seeds and place dried peppers on a hot *comal* or in a cast iron skillet for 1 minute, flipping constantly to prevent burning.
> **To reconstitute toasted peppers:** Transfer peppers to a bowl, add enough boiling hot water to cover, and soften for about 15 minutes in liquid.
> **To reconstitute dried peppers:** Place stemmed and seeded dried peppers in a saucepan with enough water to cover and bring to a boil. Lower heat and leave gently bubbling until softened, about 15 minutes.

When reconstituted, it is important to completely submerge the peppers in the hot liquid; place a small bowl over peppers to act as weight. Strain and reserve at least 1 cup of liquid to use when puréeing as well as to adjust consistency. Rinse dried peppers several times in hot boiling water to reduce the heat level in a recipe if your preference is for a milder flavor.

***Freír*, or panfrying,** is the final step to bringing the flavors in a cooked *salsa* together. Place a saucepan over medium heat, add lard or olive oil to pan, preheat 2 minutes. Remove pan from heat to minimize splattering, slowly pour in the *salsa*, return to heat and cook until simmering for a minimum of 20 minutes, unless specified.

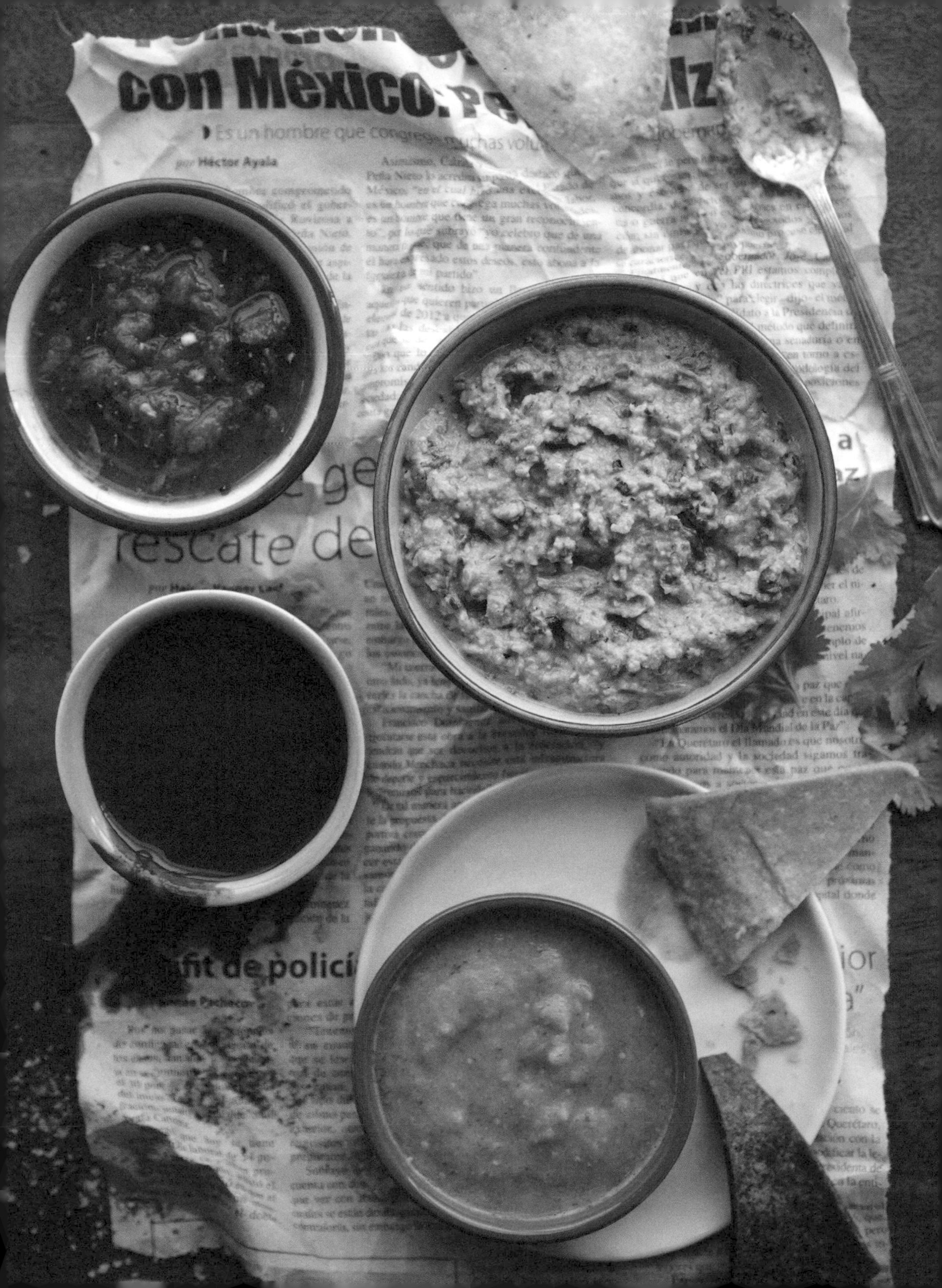
con México:
por Héctor Ayala

## Salsa tarasca
### Pumpkin Seed *and* Peanut Salsa | *Makes 2 cups*

This chunky *salsa* originates from the state of Michoacán. Its name refers to the state's indigenous people, who have lived in this region for centuries.

| | |
|---|---|
| ½ cup pumpkin seeds, hulled, roasted | 2 canned chipotle peppers in adobo, seeded |
| ½ cup peanuts, roasted | ½ medium white onion, quartered, roasted |
| 4 medium tomatoes, roasted, peeled, coarsely chopped | 5 garlic cloves, peeled, roasted |
| 2 medium *tomatillos*, husks removed, roasted, coarsely chopped | 1½ tsp kosher salt |
| | ½ small bunch cilantro, leaves only |

Place pumpkin seeds and peanuts in food processor and purée into a chunky paste. Transfer to bowl. In the same food processor, place tomatoes, *tomatillos*, peppers, onion, garlic and salt and purée into a smooth consistency. Add the chunky paste and cilantro. Pulse three times. Transfer to a bowl and serve with *totopos* (recipe below).

## Salsa de tomatillo
### Tomatillo Salsa | *Makes 1½ cups*

This *salsa* goes well on top of various *antojitos* such as *flautas* (page 45). This *salsa* is used as the base for the *guisado de cazuela de puerco con chile verde* (page 90).

| | |
|---|---|
| 4 medium *tomatillos*, husks removed, coarsely chopped | 1 tbsp finely chopped white onion |
| 1 whole *serrano* pepper, stemmed | ¼ small bunch cilantro |
| 2 garlic cloves, peeled | ½ tsp kosher salt |

Place *tomatillos*, pepper, garlic and onion in blender and purée into a smooth consistency. Add cilantro and salt; blend for only a couple of seconds in order to keep the texture of the cilantro in the *salsa*. Transfer to a bowl and serve.

## Totopos
### Freshly Made Tortilla Chips | *Makes 64 chips*

*Totopos* are accompaniments for any of the *salsas* showcased in this chapter and a great use for day-old *tortillas*.

| | |
|---|---|
| 1½ cups corn oil | Salt to taste |
| 8 regular-sized *tortillas* (page 74), cut into triangles | |

Place cast iron skillet over medium-high heat, add corn oil to skillet and preheat to bubbling, about 3 to 4 minutes. Working in batches, add *tortilla* triangles to oil and fry until crispy, about 2 minutes per side. Using a pair of tongs or a spider scoop, transfer *totopos* to paper towels to drain. Sprinkle salt.

*Pictured on opposite page, clockwise from top right: salsa tarasca, salsa de tomatillo, salsa de ajo (page 120), Hugo's salsa Mexicana (page 120)*

# Salsa de ajo
## Garlic *and* Red Chile Salsa | *Makes 2 cups*

I love the taste of garlic, especially in my *salsas*. This *salsa de ajo* is one of my favorites to go with *tacos*, *tortas* or just to munch on with *totopos*.

- 8-10 long dried *guajillo* peppers, stemmed, seeded, reconstituted (reserve ½ cup of liquid)
- 2 dried *chile de árbol*, stemmed, reconstituted

- 6 garlic cloves, peeled, roasted
- 1 tbsp finely chopped white onion
- 1¼ tsp kosher salt

Place peppers in blender along with the reserved liquid, garlic, onion and salt and purée into a smooth, thick but pourable paste. Adjust consistency by adding more reserved liquid 1 tablespoon at a time. Transfer to a bowl or store as directed on page 115. This *salsa* can also be used as a marinade as well as a topping for *tacos*.

# Hugo's salsa Mexicana
## Chunky Roasted Tomato *and* Pepper Salsa | *Makes 2 cups*

This is a basic fresh *salsa* that can be used as a dip for *totopos* or as a fresh topping on *tacos*. This *salsa* requires very little prep time and should be prepared close to serving as possible.

- ½ small white onion
- 2 garlic cloves, peeled
- 2 whole *serrano* peppers, roasted, peeled, stemmed

- ½ small bunch cilantro, divided
- 6 medium tomatoes, roasted, peeled
- 1½ tsp kosher salt

Place onion and garlic in food processor and pulse until finely chopped. Add peppers and half the amount of cilantro and pulse four times. Add tomatoes and salt and pulse four times. Transfer to bowl. Coarsely chop remaining cilantro and fold into the *salsa*. Serve with *totopos*.

*Salsa macha*

*Salsa de habanero*

*Salsa fría en molcajete*

*Chiles curtidos*

Guacamole

Salsa de jitomate y chile verde

Salsa borracha

Salsa de aguacate

# Guacamole
## Avocado Dip | *Makes 2 cups*

The secret to a good *guacamole* is to respect the avocado flavor and not to drown it in lime juice. A few drops of lime juice is more than enough for a small batch. Make just enough *guacamole* as needed. It is a simple recipe that takes just a few minutes to prepare and so another batch can be quickly made if you run out. I leave the pit in because I like the traditional, natural look it adds to the presentation.

2 tbsp finely chopped white onion
1 medium *tomatillo*, husk removed, washed, finely chopped
½ *serrano* pepper, seeded, deveined, minced
1 medium tomato, seeded, finely chopped

2 avocados, peeled, pitted, cut into large chunks
¼ small bunch cilantro, coarsely chopped
½ tsp kosher salt
¼ tsp fresh lime juice

Place onion, *tomatillo*, pepper and tomato in a colander and drain excess liquid for about 10 minutes. Place avocado chunks in mixing bowl and mash into a chunky texture. Mash gently as to leave a couple of large chunks of avocado. Fold drained ingredients into the avocado purée. Gently mix in cilantro, salt and lime juice. Transfer to bowl and accompany with *totopos*.

# Salsa macha
## Roasted Peanut *and* Tomato Salsa | *Makes 2 cups*

This spicy chunky *salsa* originated from Veracruz. Its loose translation is "she-man," alluding to the level of spiciness that characterizes this sauce.

1 tsp corn oil
3 garlic cloves, peeled, minced
½ canned chipotle pepper in adobo, seeded, deveined
1 cup dry roasted peanuts
16 dried *chile de arból* peppers, toasted

3 medium tomatoes, roasted
⅓ cup extra virgin olive oil
1 tsp dried Mexican oregano
1 tbsp lard
1½ tsp kosher salt

Place saucepan over low heat, add corn oil to pan and preheat 2 minutes. Add garlic; simmer for 15 minutes. Remove from heat and add chipotle pepper to soften in the oil-garlic mixture as it cools. Place peanuts in food processor and pulse into a chunky texture. Transfer to bowl. Place dried peppers, tomatoes and garlic-chipotle mixture in food processor. Process to a smooth purée. Add ½ cup water in a steady stream as the processor runs. Add olive oil using same method. Add crushed peanuts and oregano. Pulse to a chunky texture. Place saucepan over medium heat, add lard to pan and completely melt, preheat 2 minutes. Add *salsa macha* and cook until it thickens, about 10 minutes. Add salt. Cool completely before serving.

# Salsa borracha
### Drunken Red Chile Salsa | *Makes 1½ cups*

Traditionally, *salsa borracha* is made with *pulque*, a milk-colored alcoholic beverage made from the fermentation of the maguey and agave plant. Due to its scarcity, I used my favorite Mexican beer instead, giving it a delicious, tangy taste. This particular *salsa* will keep in the refrigerator up to three days. Store in airtight jar or plastic container.

- 6 long dried *pasilla* peppers, toasted, stemmed
- 1 cup fresh orange juice
- ¾ cup beer or 1½ cups *pulque* if available

- 5 garlic cloves, peeled
- 1 tsp kosher salt

Place peppers in a deep bowl. Add orange juice, beer or *pulque* if using, and garlic. To completely submerge peppers in liquid, place a small bowl over peppers to act as weight. Allow peppers to soften in liquid, about 1 hour. Strain, reserving 1 cup liquid, discard the rest. Transfer peppers, garlic and reserved liquid to a blender and add salt. Purée into a smooth, thick consistency. Serve with *totopos*.

# Salsa de aguacate
### Avocado *and* Tomatillo Salsa | *Makes 2½ cups*

Avocado is a delicate fruit that tends to turn brown when exposed to air. I recommend making only as much of this recipe as you can eat at one time. Prepare right before serving or up to 30 minutes prior.

- 5 medium *tomatillos*, husks removed, quartered
- ½ bunch cilantro
- ¼ large white onion
- 2 whole *serrano* peppers, roasted, stemmed, coarsely chopped

- 1 medium avocado, peeled, pitted, cut into ½-inch cubes
- 1½ tsp fresh lime juice
- 1½ tsp kosher salt

Place *tomatillos*, cilantro, onion and peppers in food processor and pulse four times. Transfer to a bowl. Fold in avocado, lime juice and salt and gently combine. Serve in small bowls and surround with *totopos* or as a topping for your choice of *tacos*.

# Salsa de jitomate y chile verde
### Tomato *and* Serrano Pepper Salsa | *Makes 2 cups*

This *salsa* is great for *enchiladas* or to give an extra kick to seafood cocktails or soups.

- 8 medium tomatoes, roasted, peeled
- 2 whole *serrano* peppers, stemmed
- 4 garlic cloves, peeled

- 1 small white onion, coarsely chopped
- ¼ cup corn oil
- 2 tsp kosher salt

Put tomatoes, peppers, garlic and onion in blender and purée to a smooth consistency. Place saucepan over medium heat, add corn oil to pan and preheat 2 minutes. Add tomato-pepper purée. Lower heat and simmer for 20 minutes. Add salt to taste. Remove from heat and cool completely before use or store as directed on page 115.

## Salsa de habanero
### Habanero Salsa | *Makes 1 cup*

*Habanero* peppers are common to the Yucatán. Since they are one of the hottest peppers in the world, I suggest wearing gloves when handling these peppers. Although I use the whole *habanero* in this recipe, you might want to remove the seeds and vein to reduce the intensity of this pepper's extreme hotness.

½ cup corn oil
1 whole *habanero* pepper, stemmed
3 garlic cloves, peeled
½ large white onion, coarsely chopped

4 medium tomatoes, roasted, peeled
½ tsp kosher salt

Place cast iron skillet over medium heat, add ¼ cup corn oil and preheat 2 minutes. Add pepper, garlic and onion and cook 5 minutes. Remove from heat and transfer to food processor or blender. Add tomatoes and process into a smooth consistency. Return skillet to medium heat, add remaining corn oil and preheat 2 minutes. Add *salsa* and salt, cook 3 minutes, stirring constantly. Remove from heat and transfer to bowl. Cool completely before serving or storing as directed on page 115.

## Salsa fría en molcajete
### Freshly Handmade Green Tomatillo Salsa | *Makes 1½ cups*

A traditional piece of equipment in *salsa* making is the three-legged mortar and pestle, or *molcajete*, made out of volcanic stone. In many Mexican households, a *molcajete* is handed down from generation to generation. Using it requires a little bit of extra elbow grease but gives a great taste when used in a recipe. It is important to add the salt to the *molcajete* before the other ingredients. It will create the necessary friction for the pestle to move more freely. I suggest serving the *salsa* in the *molcajete*, accompanied by a small wheel of *queso fresco* and warm *tortillas* as a simple and delicious appetizer. A food processor can be used as an alternative for this recipe.

1¾ tsp kosher salt
5 medium *tomatillos*, husks removed, lightly roasted, coarsely chopped
¼ small white onion, lightly roasted, coarsely chopped
2 garlic cloves, peeled, lightly roasted, coarsely chopped

1 whole *serrano* pepper, roasted, stemmed, coarsely chopped
½ medium avocado, peeled, pitted, cut into ½-inch cubes
¼ small bunch *pipicha*, optional
¼ small bunch cilantro, leaves only

Place salt on *molcajete* and mash a couple of times with the pestle. Add *tomatillos* and mash into a chunky purée. Add onion, garlic, pepper and avocado; mashing after each addition. Add *pipicha*, if using, and cilantro. If using food processor, place *tomatillos*, onion, garlic, pepper and avocado and pulse four times. The *salsa* will have a chunky texture. Add *pipicha*, if using, and cilantro and pulse twice.

## Cebolla en vinagre
### Pickled Red Onion | *Makes 2½ cups*

This recipe should be made at least one day ahead of serving, but will hold for up to two weeks in the refrigerator. It is a flavorful accompaniment and garnish to have on hand as it adds a tangy and crunchy texture — not to mention a great color accent — to *tacos*, *panuchos* and more.

| | |
|---|---|
| 1 large red onion, thinly sliced | 1 tsp dried Mexican oregano |
| 1 cup apple cider vinegar | 2½ tsp kosher salt |
| 1½ cups fresh orange juice | ½ tsp fresh ground black pepper |
| 1 tbsp fresh lime juice | |

Place onion in a deep non-corrosive container. Place saucepan over medium heat. Add vinegar, orange juice and lime juice to pan and bring to a rolling boil. Immediately remove from heat and pour over onion, making sure onion is completely submerged in liquid. Add oregano, salt and pepper, stir to combine. Allow to cool completely at room temperature. Stir occasionally. Cover and refrigerate 6 to 8 hours or up to overnight before serving. Transfer to a plastic airtight container or jar and refrigerate for up to 2 weeks.

## Chiles curtidos
### Pickled Peppers | *Makes 1 quart*

Although these are available in canned form in the Hispanic/ethnic foods aisle in local supermarkets, nothing beats homemade. *Chiles curtidos* and *cebolla en vinagre* are an accompaniment to any street food as they add a refreshing, vinegary twist. These are always in my refrigerator. In this recipe, I used red *chiles cuaresmeños*, similar to *jalapeño* peppers but a bit larger. The seeds have the same heat level but the flesh has a milder flavor, similar to that of a bell pepper. They are so named because they are eaten stuffed during lent, or *cuaresma*, a time when consuming meat is prohibited in the Catholic religion. *Jalapenõs* are a suitable alternative.

| | |
|---|---|
| 2 tbsp olive oil | 1 cup white distilled vinegar |
| 1 small white onion, sliced | 1 dried bay leaf |
| 1 garlic clove, peeled, minced | 1 tsp dried Mexican oregano |
| 1 medium carrot, peeled, sliced into medallions | 1½ tsp kosher salt |
| 10 red or green *chiles cuaresmeños* or a combination of both | |

Place saucepan over medium heat, add olive oil to pan and preheat 2 minutes. Add onion, garlic and carrot and cook for 3 minutes. Add *chiles cuaresmeños* and cook for 4 minutes. Add 2 cups water, vinegar, bay leaf and oregano and lower heat. Allow mixture to come to a slow boil, about 10 minutes. Add salt. Remove from heat and allow to cool completely at room temperature. Stir occasionally. Cover and refrigerate 6 to 8 hours or up to overnight before serving. Transfer to a plastic airtight container or jar and refrigerate for up to 2 weeks.

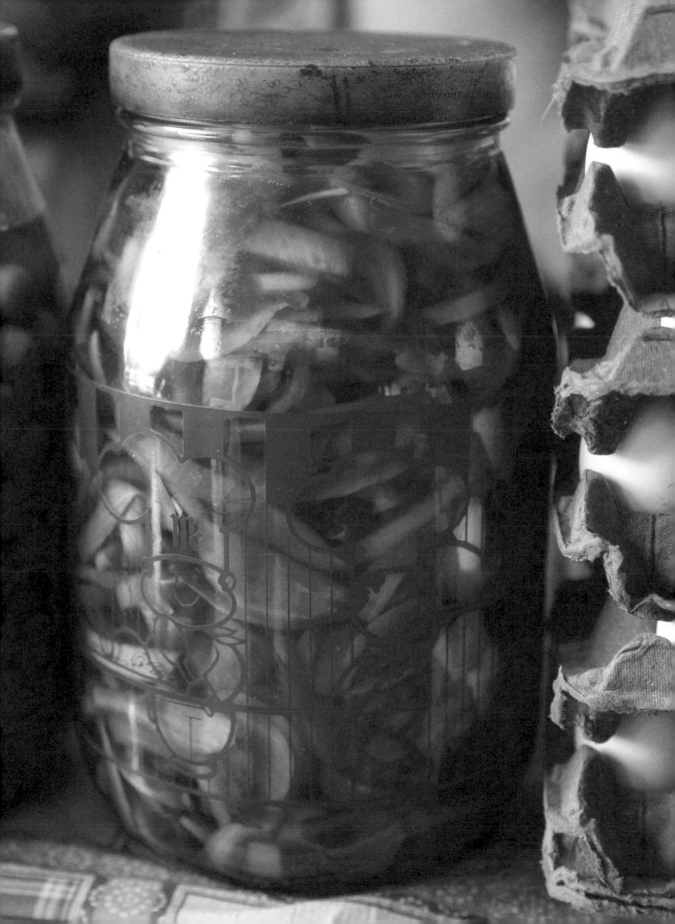

# Refritos
## Refried Beans | *Makes 3 cups*

*Refritos* — mashed beans panfried with lard — are a must-have in Mexican cooking. *Refritos* are made with black beans where I come from, but in northern Mexico, mashed pinto beans are more common. *Refritos* are traditionally made with lard but I have offered olive oil as a substitute. The wonderful thing about *refritos* is that they are always on hand in Mexican homes, used as a spread for *tortas*, *tacos* or a simple side to any meal. Mexican homecooks make three day's worth of beans, and as soon as those are done, more are made. If making ahead, allow them to completely cool, store in an airtight plastic container and refrigerate up to three days. To reheat, place a pan over medium heat, add lard or olive oil and preheat 2 minutes. Add *refritos* and simmer for 5 to 8 minutes, stirring constantly.

- 2 cups dry black beans, well rinsed
- ½ small white onion, quartered plus 1 finely chopped, divided
- 1¾ tsp kosher salt
- ⅓ cup olive oil

Place pot over medium heat, add beans, quartered onion, salt and 4 cups water to pot and bring to a boil, about 5 to 7 minutes. Lower heat and simmer until soft, about 1 hour and 30 minutes. Strain and discard liquid. Transfer beans to food processor or blender and process into a smooth purée.

Place cast iron skillet over medium heat, add olive oil to skillet and preheat 2 minutes. Add remaining onion and cook until translucent, about 3 minutes. Add purée and lower heat. Simmer for 15 minutes, stirring occasionally to prevent from sticking to pan. Remove from heat. Serve or store as mentioned above.

........................................................................................................

**Variation:** *Frijoles de olla* (Brothy Beans Cooked in a Stew Pot) Omit puréeing beans and keep liquid. Serve in soup bowls and sprinkle with *queso fresco* as garnish. Store as directed above.

# Arroz a la Mexicana
## Mexican Fried Rice | *Makes 6 servings*

This type of rice is a typical and quick side dish in Mexican homes, and a very personal one at that. Every Mexican home cook has his or her unique cooking method and ingredient list that was either passed down from generation to generation or perfected through years of trial and error. But, regardless of the origin or cook, *arroz a la Mexicana* has to meet a certain criteria, which is to showcase the three colors of the Mexican flag — green, white and red. The best thing about *arroz a la Mexicana* is there is always leftovers to use later when making your favorite *tacos*.

| | |
|---|---|
| 2 tbsp corn oil | 2 cups chicken stock |
| ½ cup finely chopped white onion | ½ cup frozen peas, thawed |
| 1 cup cubed (½-inch) carrot | ¼ cup finely chopped cilantro |
| 2 cups parboiled enriched long grain white rice | 1¼ tsp table salt |
| 1 cup coarsely chopped roasted, peeled tomatoes (about 4 medium tomatoes) | |

Place saucepan over medium heat, add corn oil to pan and preheat 2 minutes. Add onion and cook 1 minute, stir. Add carrots and cook 2 minutes, stirring constantly. Add rice and cook 3 minutes, stirring occasionally. Add tomatoes and cook 3 minutes, stirring constantly. Add stock and lower heat. Stir every 5 minutes for 15 minutes, cover after each stir. Add peas, cilantro and salt, cook 3 minutes, stirring constantly. Remove from heat and let stand, tightly covered, for 5 minutes. Fluff before serving.

....................................................................................................

**Variation:** *Arroz blanco* (White Rice with Peas and Cilantro) Omit carrots and tomatoes. Follow the rest of the cooking directions as specified above.

Tortas

**Tortas** — traditional Mexican sandwiches filled with anything from meat to vegetables to a *tamal* — are as popular to eat as *tacos*, especially on the streets in Mexico City. The most common ones are: *tortas de milanesa*, breaded thin sirloin beef filets that are panfried; and *tortas de huevo con chorizo*, a breakfast sandwich of scrambled eggs and chorizo. Each region of Mexico also claims its own specialty *tortas*, such as *cemitas poblanas* from Puebla, *tortas ahogadas* from Jalisco and *pambazo*s from Veracruz. *Tortas* are commonly served wrapped in parchment paper, making them easier to eat on the go.

Having grown up eating traditional *tortas*, I expect certain things to be in a sandwich for it to be called a *torta*. In my eyes, it has to have *refritos* spread on the inside of the bread slices to act as a condiment like mayonnaise; and avocado slices, raw onion rings, peppers of some kind whether pickled or fresh as garnishes to the main filling. Most importantly it needs to be made with the right kind of bread.

*Tortas* require a special type of bread, as opposed to the common Pullman bread used in typical American sandwiches. When I was a boy, my mother would send me into town every day for bread. I would ride my father's bike to the local *panadería*, or bakery. I remember looking like a wet noodle riding his bicycle; because it was so big, I could barely keep my balance as I rode it into town. I loved visiting the *panadería* because it gave me the opportunity to watch the *panadero* putting the bread in the oven. He used a wooden spatula with a long handle to gently slide the bread into the hot adobe oven. To this day, I love the smell and taste of freshly baked bread.

I wanted to offer a few bread recipes in this chapter, because I believe the right kind of bread is so crucial to getting the right result when making an authentic *torta*. The *teleras* (oval-shaped and fluffy buns with ridges on the top), *cemitas* (sesame seed buns), and *bolillos* (football-shaped baguettes) are the three most common breads used. Since both of us grew up eating these tasty *tortas*, it seemed only natural to ask my brother Ruben to develop these bread recipes.

He showcases simple recipes here as well as time-consuming ones but all are truly worth every bit of the extra effort. Although I recommend making your own bread, these typical breads can be found in Mexican grocery stores or *panaderías*.

# Teleras

## White Bread | *Makes 8 servings*

The oval-shaped *telera* is the first bread to come to my mind when thinking of a classic *torta*. It is probably the most common bread used throughout Mexico. I asked Ruben to develop a recipe that with one bite would bring to mind memories of eating *tortas* on the go. The *telera* is a fluffy, white bread with the traditional ridges on top. To make the two indentions, we found that using a thin rolling pin to apply pressure was the most effective way to mark the ridges. The smell of this fresh bread will immediately prompt you to crave a *torta*. I have offered a simple, quick breakfast *torta* recipe at the bottom of the page.

| | |
|---|---|
| 3¾ tsp active yeast | 5 cups all-purpose flour |
| 1 tbsp granulated sugar | 2 tsp lard |
| 1¾ tsp kosher salt | |

Place yeast in ¼ cup lukewarm water; stir to dissolve. Combine sugar and salt in a separate 1½ cups water, stir until dissolved. Using a mixer fitted with dough hook attachment, place flour in bowl. Add dissolved yeast and mix on low speed for 1 minute. Add sugar-salt water in a steady stream while mixer is on low speed. Remove from mixer and transfer to a clean work surface. Knead to form a smooth dough, about 4 to 6 minutes. Add lard and continue to knead until it incorporates with dough, about 4 minutes. Shape dough into a ball and place in a lightly oiled bowl, cover with plastic wrap. Place in a warm place and leave to rise until doubled in size, about 1 hour to 1 hour and 30 minutes.

Preheat oven to 375°F. Transfer dough to a clean work surface. Punch down and divide dough into eight equal balls; loosely cover with plastic wrap while working. Round each dough ball until no seams remain. Cover again and allow them to rest for 5 minutes. Flatten each round ball into an oval shape using the tip of your fingers. With a thin rolling pin, press down two horizontal indentions across the center. Place bread indention-side down on a parchment-lined sheet pan. Leave to rise again in a warm place for 30 to 45 minutes.

Lightly brush *teleras* with water, place in oven on the middle oven rack and bake until golden brown, about 15 to 18 minutes.

...................................................................................................

**Variation: *Torta de huevo con chorizo*** (Egg and Chorizo Sandwiches) For filling: 2 tablespoons olive oil, divided; ½ cup finely chopped white onion; 6 garlic cloves, peeled, minced; 1 ½ pound Mexican *chorizo*, casings removed; 6 eggs scrambled, fully cooked; ¾ cup *refritos* (page 132, optional); and 6 *teleras*, split-open, lengthwise. Place cast iron skillet over medium heat, add olive oil to skillet, preheat. Add onion and garlic, cook 3 minutes. Add *chorizo* and fully cook, about 20 minutes. Fold in scrambled eggs into *chorizo*. Remove from heat. Spread 2 tablespoons *refritos* on the bottom bun of each *telera*. Evenly divide egg mixture among *teleras*.

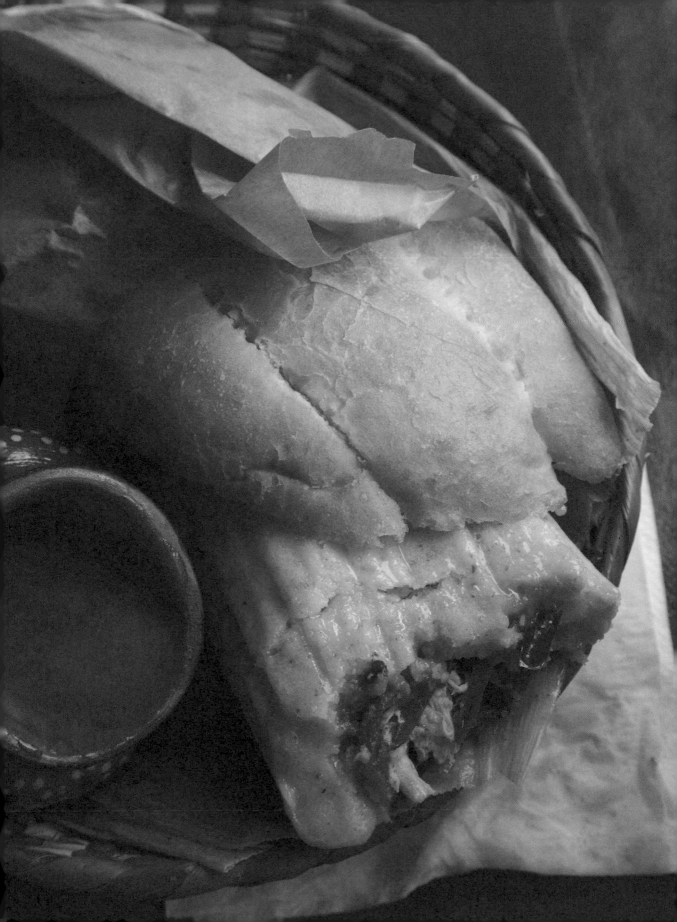

# Guajolotas
## Tamal-Stuffed Sandwiches *from* Mexico City | *Makes 6 servings*

The *guajolota* is the popular tamal-stuffed *torta* found in the streets of Mexico City. I am fortunate that when I want to make *tamales* from scratch, I can visit my local Mexican grocery store to purchase a bundle of fresh *masa para tamales* (page 248). However, it can be difficult to find in some places. *Masa para tamal* is similar to fresh *masa* (page 24) but with a coarser texture. This texture helps the *tamales* have a fluffy consistency. To simplify things, this recipe calls for instant *masa* flour for *tamales*, which is more easily found in the Hispanic/ethnic foods aisle of most supermarkets. Follow the packaged instructions, which will yield enough dough for 16 *tamales*. This recipe calls for 6 *tamales*. Freeze left over *tamales* to enjoy later.

**For *tamales*:**

1 recipe *tamal* dough (prepared from packaged directions)

1 roasted chicken (3½ lb), bone-out, shredded (about 4 to 5 cups)

1 recipe *salsa de tomatillo* (page 119)

Corn husks for wrapping as needed, soaked in warm water

4 red *jalapeño* peppers, roasted, peeled, deveined and seeded, cut into strips

4 green *jalapeño* peppers, roasted, peeled, deveined and seeded, cut into strips

**To assemble:**

6 *teleras* (page 140), split-open lengthwise

1 recipe *champurrado* (page 231), optional to accompany

**For *tamales* (make ahead up to 3 days):** Combine shredded chicken with *salsa de tomatillo* in a bowl and toss to combine. Add salt to taste. Working one at a time, drain corn husks. Place each corn husk, or two depending on size, in the palm of your hand with the point end facing away from you. Scoop ¼ cup *tamal* dough onto the center and spread into a rectangle ¾ inch from the top and ¼ inch from the bottom. Place ¼ cup chicken mixture in the center, followed by 2 red and 2 green *jalapeños* strips on top. Close and overlap flaps of husk. Finish by folding in the pointed end, forming a small bundle. Secure each bundle by loosely tying a strip of a corn husk in center. Place *tamales* in steamer basket over simmering water and cook until done, about 40 minutes to 1 hour. Cool completely before storing in a plastic food storage bag. Refrigerate or freeze until ready to use.

**To assemble:** If *tamales* are made ahead, reheat in steamer basket, 15 to 20 minutes if refrigerated or 30 to 40 minutes if frozen. Stuff each of the 6 *teleras* with a *tamal*. Wrap with parchment paper and place on warm platter. Accompany with *champurrado*.

# Tortas de milanesa
## Crispy Sirloin Filet Sandwiches | *Makes 6 servings*

The *torta de milanesa* is the most basic and common Mexican sandwich as it is a menu item in almost all *torta* stands in Mexico. This sandwich is stuffed with a crispy and delicious *milanesa,* or a thin breaded slice of beef. It is extremely filling and easy to recreate at home. Ask your butcher to thinly slice your meat or buy the pre-packaged meat for *milanesa* at local Mexican grocery stores.

**For *milanesas*:**
- 6 beef sirloin tip roast filets or *milanesas*, boneless, thinly sliced or pounded to ⅛-inch thick
- ¾ cup all-purpose flour
- 2 eggs
- ¾ cup panko bread crumbs
- ½ cup corn oil

**To assemble:**
- 6 tbsp (¾ stick) unsalted butter
- 6 *teleras* (store-bought or home-made, page 140), split-open lengthwise
- ¾ cup *refritos* (page 132)
- 2 avocados, peeled, pitted, sliced
- ¾ lb *quesillo* also known as queso Oaxaca
- 6 *chiles curtidos* (page 128), cut into strips
- 1 small white onion, cut into rings

**For *milanesas*:** Working one at a time, season each side of *milanesa* with salt and pepper. Pass each *milanesa* through the flour, beaten eggs and finally through the panko bread crumbs, shaking off excess each time. Place breaded *milanesas* on a sheet pan until ready to panfry.

Place cast iron skillet over medium heat, add corn oil to skillet and preheat to bubbling, about 3 to 4 minutes. Working one at a time, place each *milanesa* in the hot oil and fry until golden brown, 3 minutes per side. Place *milanesas* on paper towels to drain. Place in warm oven until ready to assemble.

**To assemble:** Place cast iron skillet over medium heat. Working one at a time, add 1 tablespoon butter per *telera* to skillet and completely melt. Place top and bottom slices of each *telera* in skillet and toast for 1 minute per side. Remove from heat and spread about 2 tablespoons *refritos* on each of the bottom slices. Place a *milanesa* on top of *refritos*, followed by 4 to 5 avocado slices, and a handful of *quesillo*. Finish off by putting 1 *chile curtido* and a couple of raw onion rings on each *torta*. Serve on a warm platter.

# Cemitas

## Sesame Seed Buns | *Makes 6 servings*

The bread for the *cemitas* is unique to Puebla, a state where my brother Ruben and I spent some memorable childhood years. I discovered that the recipe for these sesame seed buns is completely top secret: how it is made, shaped and baked. This recipe is Ruben's effort to recreate a bread with the perfect taste and fluffiness of the typical *torta* found in Puebla. In order to give this bread its airy and soft texture, a starter dough must be made at least one day in advance. Traditionally, this bread is made with *pulque*, a milk-colored alcoholic beverage made from the maguey and agave plant. However, as *pulque* is difficult to find, he used our favorite Mexican beer here instead.

### Starter Dough (make ahead 1 day):

½ tsp active yeast

1 cup all-purpose flour

1 tbsp *pulque* or beer

Place yeast in ⅓ cup water; stir to dissolve. Using a stand-up mixer fitted with paddle attachment, place dissolved yeast in bowl along with flour, mix on low speed for 1 minute. Add *pulque* or beer, mix on medium speed until smooth, about 2 minutes. Transfer to a bowl, cover with plastic wrap and refrigerate for 1 day. Use a kitchen scale to measure out ½ pound starter dough for recipe below. Discard any remaining.

### *Cemitas:*

4 tsp active yeast

5¼ cups all-purpose flour

½ lb Starter Dough

7 tbsp melted butter

2 tsp kosher salt

1 egg, lightly beaten mixed with 1 tbsp water

6 tbsp toasted sesame seeds

Place yeast in ¼ cup lukewarm water; stir to dissolve. Using a stand-up mixer fitted with dough hook attachment, place dissolved yeast in bowl, along with 1 ¼ cups more water, flour, starter dough, butter and salt. Mix on low speed for 2 minutes. Remove dough from mixer and transfer to a clean work surface. Knead dough until elastic, about 5 to 8 minutes. Transfer to a lightly-greased bowl and cover with plastic wrap. Place in warm place until doubled in size, about 1 hour.

Preheat oven to 375°F. Divide dough into six equal balls. Place parchment paper on a full sheet pan and apply a light mist of unflavored cooking spray. Transfer dough balls onto sheet pan. Press down on dough balls, enough to expand to match the size of your palm. Make two shallow slits along the circumference of each dough ball using a sharp knife. Place in a warm place to rise for 20 to 25 minutes.

Lightly brush each ball with egg wash and sprinkle 1 tablespoon toasted sesame seeds. Place in oven on the middle oven rack and bake until light golden brown, about 25 to 28 minutes.

# Cemitas Poblanas
## Sandwiches *from* Puebla | *Makes 6 servings*

Authentic *cemitas poblanas* are distinguished by three factors: the bread, a pungent herb called *papalo*, and the delicious, freshly made cheese strings of *quesillo* as seen on page 150. *Cemitas,* or the sesame seed buns, are stuffed with a chicken *milanesa,* a chicken breast pounded extremely thin, breaded and panfried until crispy. The herb *papalo* is a wild herb that grows in this region and is used frequently in kitchens throughout Puebla. It is available in Mexican farmers markets or specialty gourmet grocery stores. Cilantro can be used as an alternative. The flavor of cilantro is not the same as *papalo* but will add the necessary freshness as well as complement the other ingredients in the *torta.*

### For *milanesas*:
- 6 chicken breasts, pounded to ⅛-inch thick
- ¾ cup all-purpose flour
- 2 eggs, lightly beaten
- ¾ cup panko bread crumbs
- ½ cup corn oil

### To assemble:
- 6 *cemitas* (page 147), split open
- 6 tbsp mayonnaise
- ¾ cup *refritos* (page 132)
- 6 cups *quesillo* also known as queso Oaxaca
- 2 avocados, peeled, pitted, sliced
- 1 medium white onion, thinly sliced
- 6 canned chipotle peppers in adobo, seeded, sliced
- ½ bunch *papalo* or cilantro, leaves only

**For *milanesas*:** Working one at a time, season each side of *milanesas* with salt and pepper. Pass each *milanesa* through the flour, beaten eggs and finally through the panko bread crumbs, shaking off excess each time. Place breaded *milanesas* on a sheet pan until ready to panfry.

Place cast iron skillet over medium heat, add corn oil to skillet and preheat to bubbling, about 3 to 4 minutes. Working one at a time, place each *milanesa* in the hot oil and fry until golden brown, 3 minutes per side. Place *milanesas* on paper towels to drain. Place in warm oven until ready to assemble.

**To assemble:** Spread 1 tablespoon mayonnaise on the bottom slice of each *cemita* and 2 tablespoons *refritos* on the top slices. Place 1 *milanesa* for each serving; followed by a generous handful of *quesillo,* 4 to 5 avocado slices, 2 to 3 onion slices and 1 chipotle pepper. Top each *cemita* with 8 to 10 *papalos* or cilantro leaves.

Place on a warm plate and serve.

# Tortas de luchador
## Over-Stuffed Sandwiches *with* Pork | *Makes 6 servings*

There is a *torta* stand in Mexico City called *Cafetería El Cuadrilátero*, owned by a masked wrestler or *luchador* named Super Astro. He has covered his stand's walls with memorabilia from Mexico's favorite past time, *la lucha libre*. Not only that, he features a huge, platter-sized *torta* in his display window and puts the customer to the challenge: eat *El Gladiador*, the gladiator, in 15 minutes and lunch is free. I can honestly say I have never taken the challenge, but instead I developed a recipe for a sandwich fit for even the biggest wrestler. I hope you enjoy it!

**To marinate pork:**
- ¼ lb *achiote* paste
- ¼ cup orange juice
- ¼ cup chicken stock
- ¼ cup distilled white vinegar
- 2 dried *guajillo* peppers, toasted, deveined, seeded, reconstituted
- 3 garlic cloves, peeled, roasted
- ½ tsp whole cumin seeds
- ½ tsp dried thyme leaves
- 2 dried *hojas de aguacate*, optional
- 2 dried bay leaves
- ½ tsp fresh ground black pepper
- 1 tbsp kosher salt
- 1 small cinnamon stick, broken into pieces
- 1 pork butt (4 lb), bone-in

**To assemble:**
- 6 tbsp (¾ stick) unsalted butter
- 6 *teleras* (page 140), split-open lengthwise
- 12 slices *queso fresco*, ¼-inch thick by 2-inches wide and long
- 6 *chiles curtidos* (page 128), cut into slices
- ½ medium white onion, thinly sliced

**To marinate pork (make ahead up to 1 day):** Place paste, orange juice, chicken stock, vinegar, peppers and garlic in blender. Add cumin, thyme, *hojas de aguacate*, if using, bay leaves, black pepper, salt and cinnamon. Purée into a smooth consistency. Pierce pork butt several times using a sharp knife and transfer to a plastic storage bag. Pour in marinade and secure bag. Make sure marinade completely covers the meat. Place bag in pan or container and refrigerate. Allow meat to marinade for at least 2 hours or up to overnight.

**To assemble:** Preheat oven to 375°F. Transfer pork butt to a rack on a roasting pan. Cover with aluminum foil, place in oven and roast until fork tender, about 3 hours. Halfway through cooking time, remove from oven and baste with pan juices. Cover with aluminum foil when done and rest meat for 15 minutes. Debone and coarsely chop meat. Strain the pan juices and set aside.

Place a cast iron skillet over medium heat. Add 1 tablespoon butter to skillet and completely melt. Toast each *telera* top and bottom slice in the melted butter, 1 minute per side. Add more butter to pan as needed. Place about 4 to 5 ounces meat on each toasted *torta*, followed by 2 slices of *queso fresco*, 1 *chile curtido* and raw onion rings. Drizzle 1 tablespoon pan juices over the filling of each *torta de luchador* before serving. Serve on warm platter.

# Bolillos
## Hard-Crusted Sandwich Rolls | *Makes 6 servings*

We used Mexican beer for the starter dough in this recipe to recreate the light sourdough taste of an authentic *bolillo*. When incorporating the starter dough into the dough, use all of it. The dough will feel dry at first but by kneading the starter into the dough, the continuous motion will eventually give the dough elasticity. Instead of using an electric mixer, use a dough scraper to cut ingredients into the flour. This method makes the bread's texture and flavor even more delicious.

**Starter Dough (make ahead 1 day):**

1¼ cups all-purpose flour

1¼ tsp active yeast

½ cup plus 1 tbsp beer

Place flour on a clean work surface. Add yeast and using a dough scraper, cut in the flour. Gather ingredients and form into a mound. Make a well in the center and add beer, 1 tablespoon at a time. Use dough scraper to form a rough dough. Transfer to a bowl and cover with plastic. Ferment in a warm place overnight.

**Dough:**

2 cups all-purpose flour, sifted

2 tsp active yeast

2½ tbsp granulated sugar

¾ tbsp plus ½ tsp kosher salt, divided

1 recipe of Starter Dough

½ cup beer

On a clean work surface, make a mound with the flour, yeast, sugar and ¾ tablespoon salt. Add pieces of starter dough a little at a time, cutting into the flour with a dough scraper. The dough will be dry and crumbly. Add beer 1 tablespoon at a time. As the dough begins to form, continue to knead until elastic, about 15 to 20 minutes. Transfer to an oiled bowl and cover with plastic. Place in a warm place and allow it to rise until doubled in size, about 1 hour and 45 minutes.

Divide dough into six equal balls. Cup your hand and roll each ball into a football shape. Pinch down the left and right ends of each shape. Flatten each formed roll with your palm. Take each of the ends and stretch the formed roll to 6 inches in length. Slit the top of each roll with a serrated knife. Place on a parchment-lined sheet pan.

Preheat oven to 400°F. Place *bolillos* on a warm place and allow to rise for 40 more minutes. Meanwhile, dissolve remaining salt in ¼ teaspoon water. Place a sheet pan on the bottom rack of oven and fill with hot water. Carefully brush *bolillos* with the salt-water solution and place in oven on the middle oven rack. Bake until golden brown, about 20 to 25 minutes.

.....................................................................................................................

**Variation:** *Pambazos* (Hard-Crusted Bread Rolls) When shaping, flatten with the palm of your hand to expand to 4 to 5 inches in diameter. Follow the rest of the cooking directions as specified above. When placing in hot oven, dust with flour. Omit salt-water solution.

# Tortas ahogadas
## Sandwiches Drowned *in* Sauce | *Makes 6 servings*

*Torta ahogada,* or drowned, is a sandwich native to the region of Jalisco. It is quite messy to eat but extremely delicious. I made two sauces in my interpretation: a spicy one to pour over the filling and a second one to dip the bread into. The two sauces combine to form a pool on the bottom of the plate. I recommend using a spoon when eating this delicious *torta.*

**For filling:**
- 1 pork butt (3 lb), deboned, trussed
- 1 tbsp plus 1 tsp kosher salt, divided
- 1 tsp fresh ground black pepper
- 2 cups *salsa de ajo* (page 120), divided

**To assemble:**
- 6 dried *chiles de árbol* peppers, toasted, stemmed
- 4 garlic cloves, peeled, roasted
- 4 tomatoes, roasted
- ½ large white onion, roasted
- 2½ cups chicken stock
- 3 tbsp lard, divided
- ½ cup Valentina® sauce, store-bought
- 6 *bolillos* (store-bought or home-made, page 155), split-open lengthwise
- 1 small white onion, thinly sliced
- 6 *cebollitas cambray* (Mexican green onions), roasted

**For filling (make ahead up to 2 days):** Season pork butt with 1 tablespoon salt and black pepper. Transfer to a plastic food storage bag. Pour in 1 cup *salsa de ajo* and close bag, making sure the marinade covers pork butt completely. Place bag in pan or container and refrigerate for at least 2 hours or up to overnight.

Preheat oven to 325°F. Transfer pork butt to a rack on a roasting pan. Cover with aluminum foil and roast until fork tender, about 4 hours. Half way through cooking process, remove from oven and baste with pan juices. Remove from oven and allow it to rest for 15 minutes, covered. Coarsely chop meat. Place in bowl, cover with plastic and refrigerate, if making ahead.

**To assemble:** Place peppers, garlic, tomatoes, onion and chicken stock in blender and purée into a smooth consistency. Place a saucepan over medium heat, add 2 tablespoons lard and melt, preheat 1 minute. Add sauce. Reduce heat and simmer 10 minutes, stirring occasionally. Remove from heat and stir in Valentina® sauce and 1 teaspoon salt.

Place cast iron skillet over medium heat, add remaining lard and melt, preheat 2 minutes. Add pork and cook until it becomes crispy, 2 minutes, stirring occasionally. Add salt to taste. Transfer to bowl and place in warm oven until ready to assemble. Return skillet over medium heat.

Pour remaining *salsa de ajo* in bowl. Working one at a time, take each bottom and top slices of each *bolillo* and dip into *salsa de ajo*, coating both sides. Place in hot skillet and toast 1 minute per side. Place 5 ounces pork and a couple of raw onion rings on each *torta* and pour about 4 to 6 tablespoons of the freshly made *salsa* over meat and onions. Place each *torta* on a plate along with 1 roasted green onion.

# Pambazos

## Sandwiches Filled *with* Potatoes *and* Chorizo | *Makes 4 servings*

The *pambazo* is made with a round, lightly floured bread roll, which is a variation of the *bolillo* recipe on page 155. The name of this *torta* is synonymous with the bread used. The most common filling is potatoes with chorizo and can serve as a breakfast *torta*. The presentation varies, however. In central Mexico, the bread is dipped in a dried *guajillo* pepper sauce, and then pan-fried to sear in the sauce, similar to my interpretation of the *torta ahogada* (page 156). Both variations are showcased in the following recipe.

- 2 small yellow potatoes, cut in half lengthwise
- 2 garlic cloves, peeled, minced, divided
- 1 cup finely chopped white onion, divided
- 3 tbsp olive oil, divided
- 1 lb Mexican *chorizo*, casings removed
- ½ tsp kosher salt
- ½ cup *refritos* (page 132)

- 4 *pambazos* (page 155), split open
- ½ head of Napa cabbage, shredded
- 2 thinly sliced radishes
- 4 *chiles curtidos*, cut into strips (page 128)
- ½ avocado, peeled, pitted, sliced
- 4 tbsp *queso fresco*, crumbled, optional

Preheat oven to 375°F.

Place cut potatoes in bowl with 1 clove minced garlic, 2 tablespoons onion and 1 tablespoon olive oil. Toss to coat. Transfer to a sheet pan and roast for 20 minutes. Remove from oven and cool enough to handle. Cut into ½-inch cubes. Place frying pan over medium heat, pour remaining olive oil and preheat 1 minute. Add both remaining onion and garlic and cook until translucent, about 3 minutes. Add chorizo and fully cook, about 20 minutes. Add potatoes and salt. Continue cooking until potatoes are done, about 5 minutes.

Spread 2 tablespoons *refritos* on bottom slice of each *pambazo* bun. Place ½ cup filling on each, followed by a handful of shredded Napa cabbage, a pinch of radish slices, 1 sliced *chile curtido* and 2 slices of avocado. Sprinkle 1 tablespoon *queso fresco*, if using. Serve on a warm platter.

..............................................................................................

**Variation: *Pambazos Mexicanos*** (Salsa Dipped Sandwiches) For bread, pour 1 cup *salsa de ajo* (page 120) in bowl. Place cast iron skillet over medium heat, add ¼ cup lard to skillet and melt, preheat 2 minutes. Working one at a time, dip top and bottom slices of each bread in *salsa de ajo* and place on skillet. Sear in sauce for 1 minute per side. Follow the rest of cooking directions as specified above. Omit *chiles curtidos*, if desired.

# Ceviches y Cocteles

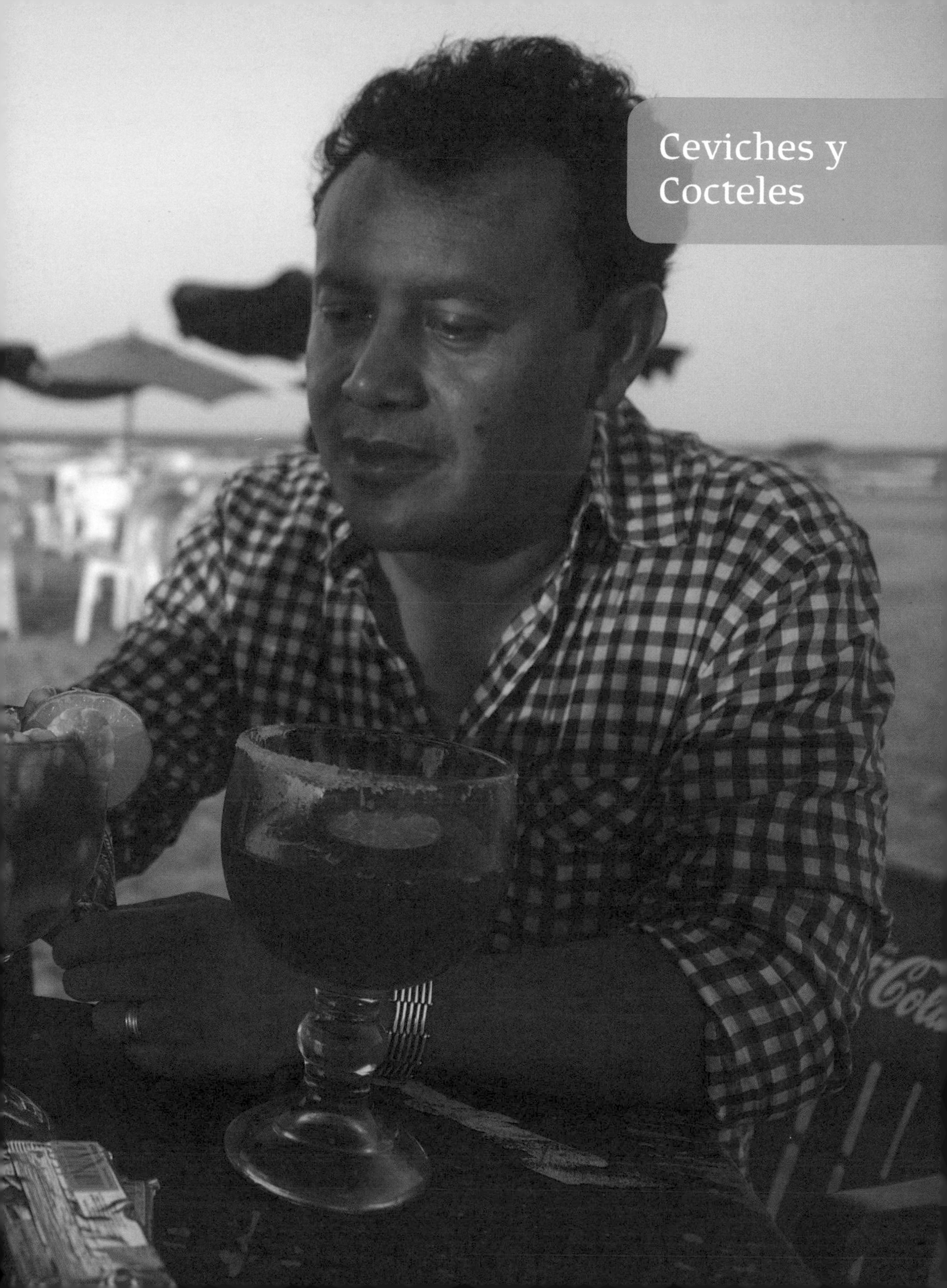

**Ceviches and cocteles** are delicious *entradas*, or appetizers, that can be found in the streets in Mexico near seafood markets and in coastal towns near the beach. *Ceviches* are fresh salads that are comprised of seafood "cooked" in lime juice for a period of time and then mixed with fresh ingredients, most commonly diced tomatoes, finely chopped white onion, cilantro and minced fresh peppers. These are served in cocktail glasses or in bowls for people to enjoy with edible utensils — like *totopos*, or saltines. *Cocteles*, or cocktails, are not drinks but seafood cooked in water, drained, cooled then commonly mixed with tomato juice, a bit of lime juice and served in cocktail glasses.

I was about nine years old when I first saw the ocean. My family and I were invited to a wedding in the port of Veracruz. After a long bus ride from Puebla, I remember stepping off the bus and being overwhelmed by the wonders of the ocean—its people, food and culture. I remember seeing the locals barefoot on the beach, selling *ceviches* and seafood cocktails and carrying fresh-caught fish tied with strands of palm leaves, yelling out "*ceviches, compre sus ceviches.*" This is a memory I cherish to this day. We had arrived a few days early because, as my mother told me, *Veracruzanos* are extremely happy people and are keen to celebrate all week long before a wedding. We went to several gatherings with live music, food and plenty of dancing. On one occasion, a local fisherman brought freshly caught snapper to the beach where we had gathered and prepared a delicious and refreshing *ceviche* — my first one — right there in front of us. After one bite, I had fallen in love.

My love grew even stronger as I had the opportunity to work in a cocktail stand in Mexico City a couple of years later. The stand also sold *pollas* — shots of sherry wine with a raw egg in it. The consumption of *pollas* and *caldo de camarón* were said to cure severe hangovers. I was too young at the time to find out whether or not this was true, but their popularity with customers was a testament to the recipe.

As the years progressed, I learned the healthy benefits of seafood and its richness in protein. I never tire of eating or preparing octopus, snapper or just about anything else from the ocean. I was given a "once-in-a-lifetime" opportunity as a child to be shown what the ocean has to offer. Seeing how seafood can be marinated in lime juice, combined with fresh ingredients and turned into a refreshing and wonderful *ceviche* still captivates me. I truly believe this is "food from the Gods."

# Ceviche de huachinango
## Red Snapper Ceviche | *Makes 4 servings*

The following recipe celebrates my first taste of *ceviche* from that wonderful day in Veracruz when family and friends gathered for a memorable wedding celebration. In this recipe, I used red snapper. If preferred, substitute salmon, grouper, tilapia or halibut. Fish is "cooked" when it is white and no longer translucent, and feels firmer to the touch.

| | |
|---|---|
| 6 oz red snapper, cut into ½-inch cubes | 1 tbsp pitted green olives, sliced |
| 1 tbsp finely diced white onion | 1½ tsp olive oil |
| ¾ cup fresh lime juice | ½ tsp sea salt |
| 1 tomato, seeded and finely chopped | ½ avocado, peeled, pitted and diced plus 8 slices for garnish, divided |
| ½ *jalapeño* pepper, seeded, deveined and minced | 1 recipe *totopos* (page 119), optional to accompany |
| 2 tbsp chopped cilantro plus 4 sprigs for garnish, divided | |

Combine snapper, onion and lime juice in glass or ceramic bowl. Make sure snapper floats freely in lime juice to ensure thorough and even marinating. Cover with plastic wrap and refrigerate for 1 hour and 30 minutes. Strain and discard lime juice.

In separate bowl, combine tomato, pepper, chopped cilantro, olives and olive oil, toss to combine. Add snapper and salt, toss. Fold in diced avocado before serving. Serve in four chilled martini glasses. Garnish and serve. Accompany with *totopos*.

# Aguachile

## Shrimp Marinated *in* Lime Juice | *Makes 4 servings*

In Baja California, I found an exciting hidden treasure in the port of Ensenada — *el mercado negro*, or "Black Market," an open-air seafood market where local fishermen give samples of the freshest catch-of-day. *Aguachile* is a popular local dish in Ensenada that is sold at many of the market's *puestos*. It is a delicious *ceviche* of butterflied shrimp marinated in lime and accompanied with cucumber slices, which serve the role of the *totopos*. To butterfly the shrimp, use a sharp paring knife. Fill two small bowls with water. As you butterfly the shrimp, place shrimp in the first bowl and remove vein. Transfer to the second bowl and rinse. Then, place on paper towels to drain. Make sure shrimp is completely dry before adding the lime juice to prevent diluting the marinade.

| | |
|---|---|
| 1 lb medium shrimp, peeled, deveined, butterflied and dry | 1¼ tsp Mexican chili powder, divided |
| ¾ cup fresh lime juice | ¼ tsp dried Mexican oregano, crumbled |
| 1 tbsp finely chopped white onion | ½ cucumber |
| 1 tbsp fresh key lime juice | |
| ½ tsp sea salt plus more as needed | |

Place shrimp in glass or ceramic bowl. Add lime juice. Make sure shrimp floats freely in lime juice to ensure thorough and even marinating. Cover with plastic and refrigerate for 12 to 15 minutes. Strain and discard lime juice. Transfer shrimp to clean glass bowl. Add onion and key lime juice, toss to coat. Add salt, 1 teaspoon chili powder and oregano, toss to combine. Chill before serving.

Slice cucumber at a 45-degree angle, about ¼ inch thick. Arrange along the edge of a large platter. Sprinkle with salt and remaining chili powder. Place *aguachile* in center. Pour remaining juices over cucumbers. Serve with extra cucumber slices and saltines on a separate plate to accompany. Garnish with thinly sliced radish, red onion and lime wedges to add color.

# Coctel de jaiba
## Crab Cocktail | *Makes 6 servings*

This recipe was inspired by the beautiful blue crabs of Bahia Kino, or Kino Bay, located in the state of Sonora. These blue crabs are exceptionally large with sweet meat of very high quality that is served there in stews or *cocteles*. In this recipe, I call for the lump crabmeat that is sold in plastic tubs and has been shelled and cleaned. It is still important, however, to transfer the meat to a mixing bowl before using and to carefully run your fingers through it to see if any pieces of shell or cartilage have been left behind. Another ingredient, *xoconostle*, offers an additional flavor profile to the *coctel*. *Xoconostle* is a sour prickly pear typically used in Mexican cooking for *salsas* and can be found in selective Mexican farmers markets or in the produce section of Mexican grocery stores.

½ medium *nopal* (cactus paddle), cleaned and diced

1 tbsp kosher salt

¼ small *jicama*, peeled and diced

1 small *xoconostle*, peeled and cut into thin strips, optional

2 tbsp finely chopped white onion

1½ tbsp finely chopped cilantro

1 tomato, seeded and finely chopped

½ whole *serrano* pepper, stemmed, minced

¼ cup fresh orange juice

2 tbsp fresh lime juice

1½ tsp olive oil

1 tsp sea salt

½ lb lump crabmeat, cleaned and picked through for cartilage and pieces of shell

1 recipe *totopos* (page 119), optional to accompany

Place saucepan over high heat, add 5 cups water and kosher salt to pan and bring to a boil. Remove from heat and add *nopal*. Blanch 3 minutes. Strain immediately. Leave straining for 10 minutes to assure it is completely dry.

Place the cooked cactus paddle into a glass bowl. Add jicama, *xoconostle*, onion, cilantro, tomato and pepper. Pour in orange and lime juices and olive oil, mix. Fold in crabmeat. Mix gently as to not break apart crabmeat. Chill before serving. Divide mixture evenly among six cocktail glasses or in large bowl. Accompany with *totopos* or saltines.

# Coctel a la campechana
## Seafood Cocktail | *Makes 4 servings*

From the port of Veracruz, I bring you my interpretation of this famous cocktail. The *coctel a la campechana* is a cold seafood cocktail made with a mixture of the freshest catch-of-the-day in a spicy tomato sauce. In one of our travels to Mexico, Ruben and I met a wonderful chef/restaurant owner named Tomasita, who introduced us to this cocktail. That day, the *campechana* included octopus, conch, fish, oysters, crabmeat and clams, accompanied with freshly made *totopos*. In the background, we had a *conjunto jarocho*, a group of musicians, singing sonnets for which they ad-libbed the lyrics to tell a different story about each guest in the restaurant. When they got to us, they composed a song about our coming from Houston and passing by Veracruz. It was a wonderful and fun experience. Prepare this recipe using your choice of the freshest seafood available.

- 4 oz raw red snapper, cut into ½-inch cubes
- 1 tbsp finely chopped white onion
- ¾ cup fresh lime juice, divided
- ½ cup thinly sliced octopus (cooked and sliced according to page 176)
- 4 medium shrimp (cooked according to page 179)
- ½ cup crabmeat, cleaned and picked through any cartilage or shell pieces
- 4 oysters, shucked
- 1 tomato, seeded and finely chopped
- 2 tbsp pitted green olives, sliced
- 2 tbsp finely chopped cilantro
- 2 tbsp Valentina® sauce, store-bought
- ½ cup *salsa de jitomate y chile verde* (page 125)
- ¾ tsp sea salt
- ¼ tsp freshly ground black pepper
- 1 avocado, peeled, pitted and diced
- 1¼ cups tomato juice, chilled
- 1 recipe *totopos* (page 119), optional to accompany

Combine snapper, onion and ½ cup lime juice in glass or ceramic bowl. Make sure snapper floats freely in lime juice to ensure thorough and even marinating. Cover with plastic wrap and refrigerate for 1 hour and 30 minutes. Strain and discard lime juice.

Transfer snapper to glass bowl. Add octopus, shrimp, crabmeat and oysters and remaining lime juice, toss to combine. Add tomato, olives and cilantro, mix. Add Valentina® sauce and *salsa de jitomate y chile verde*, mix. Add salt and black pepper and lightly toss. Fold in avocado right before serving.

Divide chilled tomato juice evenly among four cocktail glasses. Divide seafood mixture evenly into the glasses. Accompany with *totopos* or saltines.

# Coctel de pulpo
## Octopus Cocktail | *Makes 4 servings*

I wanted to make a *coctel* in which the ingredients complemented the meaty flavor and texture of the octopus. When cooking the octopus, remember to remove it from the hot liquid as soon as it feels tender. This cocktail is great served in individual portions or in a large bowl for parties. If making for a party, cook the octopus up to one day ahead. Slice, place in a bowl, cover with plastic and refrigerate. Use this technique for cooking octopus in the other recipes in this chapter that call for cooked octopus.

### To cook octopus:
- ¼ cup kosher salt
- 5 dried bay leaves
- ½ large white onion, coarsely chopped
- 6 garlic cloves, peeled
- ½ large carrot, peeled, coarsely chopped
- 1 celery stalk, coarsely chopped
- 1 octopus (3 lb)

### To assemble:
- 2 tbsp finely chopped onion
- ½ tomato, seeded and finely chopped
- 1 whole *serrano* pepper, stemmed, minced
- ¼ cup chopped cilantro
- ¼ cup tomato juice, chilled
- 1 tbsp fresh lime juice
- 1 tsp Valentina® sauce, store-bought
- 1½ tbsp olive oil, divided
- ¼ tsp sea salt
- ¼ avocado, peeled, pitted and diced
- 1 recipe *totopos* (page 119), optional to accompany

**To cook octopus (make ahead up to 1 day):** Place stockpot over high heat and add salt, bay leaves, onion, garlic, carrot and celery to stockpot with about 1 ½ gallons water. Bring to a boil and continue boiling for 5 minutes. Add octopus, lower heat and leave gently bubbling until tender, about 1 hour. Remove octopus from water and transfer to a sheet pan. Allow it to cool at room temperature, about 30 to 40 minutes. Remove head from octopus and discard. Thinly slice tentacles into ¼-inch thick medallions. Refrigerate octopus covered with plastic wrap until ready to assemble.

**To assemble:** Place onion in glass bowl. Add tomato, pepper, cilantro, tomato and lime juices, Valentina® sauce, olive oil and salt. Mix to incorporate. Add chilled octopus and avocado just before serving. Divide mixture evenly into four cocktail glasses or place in large bowl. Serve cold and accompany with *totopos;* garnish with lime wedges and cilantro leaves.

# Coctel de camarón
## Shrimp Cocktail | *Makes 4 servings*

In my interpretation of a shrimp cocktail, I wanted to keep the integrity of the shrimp flavor by having the other ingredients complement it rather than drown it. Cocktail shrimp is available deveined, peeled and tail off. However, for the freshest and best flavor I suggest buying the shrimp in their shells and deveining and peeling them after cooking. Use the technique for cooking the shrimp given here in the other recipes in this chapter calling for cooked shrimp. Do not discard shrimp shells but refrigerate or freeze in a plastic bag to use for making fish stock at another time (page 191).

**To cook shrimp:**

| | |
|---|---|
| 1 garlic clove, peeled | 2 tbsp black peppercorns |
| ¼ small white onion, coarsely chopped | 2 tsp kosher salt |
| ½ celery stalk, coarsely chopped | 20 cocktail-sized shrimp |

**To assemble:**

| | |
|---|---|
| 1 tbsp finely chopped white onion | 1 tsp Valentina® sauce, store-bought |
| 1 tbsp finely diced tomato | 1 tsp lime juice |
| 1 tbsp cucumber, peeled, seeded and cut into small dice | 1½ tsp olive oil |
| 1 tbsp *jicama*, peeled and finely diced | 1 avocado slice, small dice |
| 1 tsp finely chopped cilantro | 1 tsp ketchup |
| | 1⅓ cups tomato juice, chilled |

**To cook shrimp:** Set up an ice bath by filling a bowl with ice and water. Place stockpot over high heat and add garlic, onion, celery, peppercorns, salt and 8 cups water. Bring to a rolling boil. Add shrimp and cook for 2 minutes. Immediately transfer cooked shrimp to ice bath to stop cooking process. Allow shrimp to cool completely before peeling and deveining them. Refrigerate covered with plastic wrap until ready to assemble.

**To assemble:** Transfer shrimp to glass bowl. Add onion, tomato, cucumber, *jicama* and cilantro, and toss to combine. Add Valentina® sauce, lime juice, olive oil and ketchup, mix. Fold in avocado right before serving. Pour ⅓ cup tomato juice into each of four cocktail glasses. Divide cocktail mixture evenly among cocktail glasses. Serve chilled and accompany with saltines.

# Ensalada de jumiles con nopales
## Fresh Crawfish *and* Cactus Paddle Salad | *Makes 6 servings*

This fresh crawfish salad was inspired by my childhood visits to Atlixco, the capital city of the state of Puebla. I remember eating this aromatic, refreshing *ensalada de jumiles con nopales* from a plastic bag using a plastic fork as I walked through the market with my mother. Most importantly, I remember the strong, fresh smell of the cilantro in this salad. I highly recommend using fresh crawfish when in season. When unavailable, domestic frozen crawfish tailmeat can be used.

| | |
|---|---|
| 4 small *nopales* (cactus paddles), cleaned, sliced into short, thin strips | 3 *chiles curtidos* (page 128), seeded, cut into thin strips |
| 1⅓ tbsp kosher salt, divided | ½ cup chopped cilantro |
| 1 lb fresh *jumiles* (crawfish meat), pre-cooked or frozen crawfish tail meat, thawed, drained | ½ cup fresh lime juice |
| | 1 tsp dried Mexican oregano, crumbled |
| ½ white onion, sliced into thin strips | 2 thinly sliced radishes |
| 1 tomato, seeded, cut into strips | 1 recipe *totopos* (page 119), optional to accompany |

Place saucepan over high heat, add 5 cups water and 1 tablespoon salt to pan and bring to a boil. Remove from heat and add *nopales*. Blanch 3 minutes. Strain immediately. Leave straining for 10 minutes to assure they are completely dry.

Place *jumiles* in a mixing bowl with the cooked *nopales*, onion, tomato and *chiles curtidos*, toss to combine. Add cilantro, lime juice, oregano, radishes and remaining salt and toss to combine. Divide salad evenly among six bowls. Accompany with *totopos*.

# Michelada con camarones
## Spicy Beer Cocktail *with* Shrimp | *Makes 4 servings*

In San Adrés Cholula in Puebla, Tak & Beer, a bar/*clamatería* — cocktail stand — serves an incredible spicy beer cocktail with shrimp. A tomato juice mix is poured about halfway in a mug that has a chili powder rim. A shrimp "skewer" is placed on top and a nice, cold beer is served on the side. The customer pours the beer in the mug until it fills up, replenishing the beer content after each sip. What a great way to enjoy the afternoon!

**For cocktail mix:**
- ¾ cup tomato juice, chilled
- ¼ cup fresh orange juice
- ½ cup plus 1 tbsp fresh lime juice, divided
- 1 tbsp *salsa inglesa* (Worcestershire sauce)
- ¼ tsp kosher salt
- ¾ tsp ground black pepper
- 1 garlic clove, peeled
- ½ whole *serrano* pepper, stemmed
- 1½ cup Clamato® tomato cocktail juice, store-bought, chilled

**To assemble:**
- Fresh lime juice as needed
- ¼ cup Mexican chili powder
- 4 beer mugs, chilled
- 4 long bamboo toothpicks
- 24 medium shrimp (cooked according to page 179)
- 4 cold dark beers

**For cocktail mix:** Pour tomato, orange and 1 tablespoon lime juices in blender. Add *salsa inglesa*, salt, ground black pepper, garlic and pepper. Purée into a smooth consistency. Transfer to pitcher. Add Clamato® juice and remaining lime juice, stir to combine.

**To assemble:** Pour a small amount of fresh lime juice onto a small plate; place chili powder on a separate small plate and form into a mound. Working one at a time, dip the rim of each beer mug in the lime juice and transfer to the chili powder, creating a red ring on each.

Divide cocktail mix evenly among beer mugs. Skewer 6 shrimp onto each toothpick and place 1 skewer on top of each mug. Serve with beer.

# Ostiones en la playa
## Shucked Oysters *with* Hot Sauce *and* Lime | *Makes 4 servings*

In my most recent visit to Veracruz, a friend, Marín Gutiérrez (pictured on the following pages), drove my brother and me to a secluded beach, *Playa Norte* — a quiet, peaceful beach visited by the locals trying to escape the tourist-filled streets. We bought oysters, fresh-caught fish and vegetables at the *mercado* and took them to the beach for a relaxing dinner outdoors. As we shucked oysters, cooked the fish over the coals and walked barefoot on the beach, it brought back my fondest memory of that first time I saw the ocean so many years ago.

24 to 28 fresh oysters
½ cup Valentina® sauce, store-bought

4 tbsp finely chopped cilantro
12 *limones criollos* (key limes), sliced into wedges

Check freshness of oysters. Oyster shell must be tightly closed; discard any that have an opened shell. Place oysters under running water and brush off any excess dirt. Work over a bowl or sink to catch juices. Use a towel to hold the oyster in the palm of your hand. Make sure flatter side of oyster is facing up and the cup-side down. Working one at a time, insert paring knife or oyster knife at the hinge of each oyster. Twist knife to remove top shell. Remove meat from shell into bottom shell. Place oysters on the half-shell on large platter.

Drizzle 1 teaspoon Valentina® sauce on each. Sprinkle chopped cilantro throughout oysters. Squeeze one lime wedge on each and serve oysters immediately.

Accompany with cold beers.

# Caldo de camarón
## Fortified Shrimp Soup | *Makes 8 servings*

Every *coctelería* in Mexico offers *caldo de camarón*, a spicy shrimp soup that is thought to be a perfect cure for a hangover. During the weekends, people especially visit their local seafood cocktail stand and ask for *caldo de camarón* to lift up their spirits. It is commonly served in a shot glass, just the right amount necessary to wake up the senses. Serve the *caldo de camarón* in soup bowls or small shot glasses for a party as a fun appetizer. Dried shrimp is naturally salty and available in the spice aisle in Mexican or Asian grocery stores. For the fish stock in this recipe, visit your local seafood market to purchase fish bones and heads. Reserve the shrimp shells from previous use and add to stock to fortify the flavor.

**Fish stock:**
- 1 lb bones from lean fish or 2 fish heads
- 1 small onion, coarsely chopped
- 1 celery stalk, coarsely chopped
- 1 medium carrot, peeled, coarsely chopped
- 2 small dried bay leaves

**For soup:**
- ½ cup dried shrimp, store-bought
- 5 tomatoes, roasted, peeled
- 3 dried *ancho* peppers, toasted, seeded, deveined and reconstituted
- 3 dried *pulla* or *guajillo* peppers, toasted, seeded, deveined and reconstituted
- 8 garlic cloves, peeled, roasted
- ½ large white onion, roasted
- 1 tbsp fresh thyme
- 6 *epazote* leaves
- 2 dried bay leaves
- ¼ cup olive oil
- 4 cups Clamato® tomato cocktail juice, store-bought
- ¼ cup fresh lime juice

**Fish stock:** Place bones, fish heads and/or shrimp shells, if using, onion, celery, carrot and bay leaves in a large stockpot. Add enough water to cover, about 8 cups. Place pot over high heat and bring to a boil. Reduce heat to medium and simmer stock for 45 minutes to 1 hour. Strain and discard bones. Set stock aside until ready to use.

**For soup:** Place a cast iron skillet over low heat and preheat 5 minutes. Add dried shrimp to skillet and toast, 1 minute per side. Transfer to a blender along with tomatoes, peppers, garlic, onion and purée into a smooth consistency. Add thyme, *epazote* and bay leaves and purée once more.

Place a saucepan over high heat, add olive oil to pan and preheat 30 seconds. Add the purée and stir for 10 minutes. Lower heat to medium and reduce into a paste, about 10 minutes, stir occasionally. The paste will be ready when it begins to slightly stick to pan. Add stock, Clamato® and lime juices and bring to a boil. Remove from heat and allow it to sit for 5 minutes. Add salt to taste.

Serve *caldo de camarón* in soup bowls or in shot glasses with lime wedges as garnish.

Dulces

# Dulces

**Dulces** — sweets, pastries, candies and frozen treats — are delicious, vibrant indulgences that can be found in the streets at stands in the market or from a cart pushed by a vendor. *Dulces* are also made and sold at the *panadería*, Mexican bakery. I love desserts and chocolate making, but due to the constant demands of running our restaurants' kitchens, I can honestly say that I know how to make only one dessert. I have been lucky to have my *carnalito* — Spanish slang for "little brother" — Ruben, working with me. He has a natural talent for dessert making. While I have been working on the savory side of the kitchen, Ruben has always had full charge of dessert development. Ruben is the pastry chef for both Backstreet Cafe and Hugo's. His first pastry job was at Backstreet back in 1993 and he took part in the opening of Hugo's by developing the dessert menu. He has worked closely with me ever since. It seemed only natural to me to ask him to share his recipes here.

Being in the restaurant business, it is good to work with someone that knows you well. The foundation of my relationship with Hugo is that we are brothers. We have also grown a close bond of friendship from almost 20 years of working together. We are many things: brothers, colleagues and friends. However, our role of friends always comes first. I was honored when Hugo asked me to share my recipes for *Dulces*. I chose recipes that represent our shared childhood in Mexico as well as our culture. I have included recipes from each category of Mexican sweets: pastries, candies and frozen delights.

The goal of these dessert recipes is to remind people from my country of their childhood with just one bite. When we were kids, I remember running to the door when I heard the vendor with his basket full of *cuernitos rellenos* — cornucopias filled with pastry cream — or *gaznates* — windpipe-shaped pastries filled with meringue — passing on the street in front of our house. Things have changed since those days. When I go back and visit beautiful Mexico, I see many of the sweets have become more contemporary, less traditional. However, I am relieved to see that the "good old classics" remain, and these are the ones to celebrate here. Mexican sweets are very vibrant in color due to the use of food coloring. I am not particularly fond of using artificial means to add color to food but in keeping with tradition, I implemented it in the recipes. It is, of course, always optional.

— **Ruben Ortega**

# Tamales de dulce
## Sweet Tamales *with* Rum Raisins | *Makes 16-20 pieces*

The best dessert in our house growing up was a nice, hot *tamal de dulce* straight out of the *tamalera* — a Mexican steamer specifically designed to make *tamales* — and a rich cup of hot chocolate. In this recipe, I included one of my favorite additions, rum-soaked raisins. Rum is a popular ingredient in Mexican desserts, and I try to use it in my recipes as much as possible. In this recipe, it gives an extra twist to my mother's memorable *tamales de dulce*. To make this recipe successfully, I have called for *masa harina para tamales* (page 248), to give just the right level of sweetness and lard to ensure a fluffy *tamal*.

**For *tamales*:**

- ½ cup raisins
- 3 tbsp white rum
- 3 cups *masa harina para tamales*
- 2 tsp baking powder
- 1¼ cups granulated sugar
- 1 cup lard
- ¼ tsp kosher salt
- 2 tsp vanilla extract
- 6 drops red food coloring, optional
- Corn husks as needed, softened in warm water

**To serve:**

1 recipe *chocolate caliente* (page 231), optional to accompany

**For *tamales*:** Place raisins, rum and ½ cup water in a small saucepan over high heat. Bring to a full boil. Remove immediately from heat. Strain raisins and transfer to a bowl to cool completely before using.

Using a mixer fitted with paddle attachment, add *masa harina para tamales*, baking powder, sugar, lard, salt, vanilla and food coloring, if using, into the bowl. Mix on medium speed for 1 minute to incorporate ingredients. While on medium speed, add 2 cups water in a steady stream. Increase speed to high and mix for 6 minutes. Test readiness of *masa* according to directions on page 248. Fold in raisins.

Working one at a time, place each corn husk, or two depending on size, in the palm of your hand with the point end facing away from you. Scoop ¼ cup *masa* onto the center and spread into a rectangle, ¾ inch from the top and ¼ inch from the bottom. Fold in the sides of the husk to the center, enclosing the *masa*. Fold up the point, forming a small bundle. Secure each bundle by loosely tying a thin strip of husk around the center of the *tamal*. Place *tamales* in steamer, covered with a clean, damp kitchen towel then the lid, and cook about 40 minutes to 1 hour.

**To serve:** Place warm *tamales* on a platter and accompany with *chocolate caliente*.

# Churros

**Mexican Fritters** | *Makes 24-30 pieces*

*Churros* are deep-fried, stick-thin fritters dredged in sugar. They are a staple Mexican street sweet. Since 1935, *churrería El Moro* has been snuggled in slot #42 on *Eje Central* and *Lázaro Cárdenas* in Mexico City. The chiseled stone sign at the door, open kitchen and smell of freshly made *churros* all play a role in this *churrería's* ever popular business (page 200). Lining one of its walls is a large vat of hot oil with a pump attached overhead. The *churrero* pulls down the lever, piping the batter as it creates a large, snake-like coil of 6 to 8 circular orbits in the hot oil. After frying, he takes two long metal skewers to pull the coil out and flip it to fry the other side. Using the same skewers, the *churros* are lifted out and placed on a large, round sheet pan, cut into portions, and dredged in sugar. For this recipe, I suggest using a household deep fryer for the best results. If unavailable, fill ¾ of a Dutch oven or pot with corn oil and attach a candy/deep fryer thermometer to the rim of the pot to control the oil temperature. Always use extreme caution when working with the hot oil.

**For batter:**
- 1 cinnamon stick
- ½ tsp vanilla extract
- 6 tbsp (¾ stick) unsalted butter or margarine
- ½ tsp kosher salt
- 2¼ cups all-purpose flour, sifted
- 1 egg

**To assemble:**
- 10 to 12 cups corn oil for deep-frying
- 1 cup granulated sugar
- ½ tsp ground cinnamon
- 1 recipe *chocolate caliente* (page 231), optional to accompany

**For batter:** Combine 2 ¼ cups water with cinnamon stick, vanilla, butter and salt in a medium saucepan. Place pan over medium heat and bring to a boil. Remove from heat and discard cinnamon stick. Add flour all at once. Stir dough using a wooden spoon until it forms into a ball, about 2 minutes. Transfer dough to a mixer fitted with paddle attachment. While on medium speed, add egg to dough and mix to incorporate. The dough will be sticky. Transfer to a pastry bag with a large star tip, suggested tip #846. Set filled pastry bag aside until ready to pipe.

**To assemble:** Pour corn oil in Dutch oven or electric fryer and preheat to 375°F. Meanwhile, combine sugar and cinnamon in a bowl and set aside. Working in batches, pipe two to three *churros* about 4 inches long into the hot oil. Completely submerge the *churros* into the hot oil by pressing down with a slotted spoon or spider and fry until golden brown, about 2 minutes. The oil will sizzle as you completely submerge the *churros*; this will help them puff up. Place fried *churros* on paper towels to drain. Transfer to sugar-cinnamon mixture and dredge, shaking off excess.

Serve four to five *churros* per person or on a large platter. Accompany with *chocolate caliente*.

# Helados Mexicanos
## Mexican Ice Creams | *Makes 1 to 1½ quarts*

*Helados* or *nieves de garrafa* are traditional Mexican ice creams and sorbets that are sold in markets throughout Mexico. The following traditional method is still used in Oaxaca. A *garrafa* machine is comprised of two parts: a wooden bucket filled with ice, water and salt and a stainless steel container that holds the ice cream/sorbet mix. The vendor places the stainless steel container inside the bucket and spins it, creating the necessary friction to turn it into a frozen treat.

| | |
|---|---|
| 2½ cups heavy cream | 1 batch flavoring as specified below |
| 2½ cups whole milk | |
| 1¼ cups granulated sugar, divided | Food coloring as needed, optional |
| 8 egg yolks | Add-ins, optional |

Combine cream, milk and half the amount of sugar in a medium saucepan over medium heat. Stir to combine ingredients, making sure sugar does not stay at the bottom of pan. Bring to a boil, about 10 minutes. Remove from heat and steep for 5 minutes.

In a separate bowl, whisk together yolks and remaining sugar until thick and pale. Temper yolks by slowing whisking in ½ cup hot cream-milk mixture. Gradually add remaining mixture to yolks in a steady stream, whisking vigorously. Return to heat and cook to 180 degrees on a thermometer or until mixture coats the back of spoon. Strain into bowl, add batch of flavoring and food coloring, if using. Place bowl in ice bath, cool and refrigerate 3 hours.

Pour base into ice cream/sorbet maker and follow manufacturer's instructions. Place ice cream in a bowl and fold in any optional add-ins. Then, place in freezer for at least 4 hours or up to overnight before serving.

### *Sabores* (Flavorings)

**Ron con pasas *(Rum with Raisins, pictured right)*:** ¾ cup raisins, ¾ cup white rum, 2 teaspoons vanilla extract and 2 drops yellow food coloring, optional. Place raisins and rum in saucepan and place over high heat. Bring to a rolling boil. Immediately remove from heat and transfer to an airtight plastic container and refrigerate overnight. Strain and reserve 2 tablespoons liquid to use with vanilla as the flavoring. Set aside raisins until ready to fold in. Follow the base and freezing directions from the master recipe.

**Chocolate *(Chocolate)*:** 2 tablets (3 oz each) Mexican *chocolate*, coarsely chopped, 1 teaspoon vanilla extract. Add *chocolate* to ice cream base while still warm, whisk to dissolve. Follow the base and freezing directions from the master recipe.

**Nuez *(Pecan)*:** ½ cup raw pecans, ½ teaspoon vanilla extract. Preheat oven to 325°F. Place pecans in single layer on sheet pan and place in oven. Roast for 8 minutes. Transfer to bowl and cool completely. Transfer pecans to blender with 2 cups cold ice cream base, process into chunky texture. Fold into the rest of ice cream base with the vanilla. Follow the base and freezing directions from the master recipe.

**Café *(Coffee)*:** ½ cup good-quality coffee beans, 1 cinnamon stick. Place beans in spice grinder or food processor and coarsely chop. Boil beans and cinnamon stick with heavy cream, milk and half amount of sugar. Strain. Follow the remaining base and freezing directions from the master recipe.

Nieve de mango

Nieve de lima

Nieve de mamey

Nieve de jamaica

*Helado de chocolate*

# Nieves Mexicanas
## Mexican Sorbets | *Makes 1 to 1½ quarts*

Fruit purées are available in specialty grocery stores, especially in baking and candy-making stores. I like using them because it is easier to control yield and sweetness levels when making a fruit sorbet. If using fresh fruit, adjust sugar accordingly. The beautiful thing about sorbets or *nieves* is their versatility to adapt to any fruit. Sorbets are usually sold from the same vendors as the *helados* or ice creams in *garrafas*, (page 202). They are a refreshing treat at the markets, especially during the hot, summer months.

**For base:**
- 2 cups granulated sugar
- ¼ cup light corn syrup

**For flavoring:**
- 2 to 4 cups fruit purée of choice
- 2 drops or as needed food coloring, optional
- ½ cup add-ins of choice, optional

**For base:** Combine sugar, corn syrup and 2 cups water in a medium saucepan. The mixture should resemble wet sand. Place saucepan over medium to high heat and bring to a boil. Continue boiling until the mixture reaches syrup consistency, about 10 minutes. Remove from heat and transfer to bowl.

**For flavoring:** Pour 1 ½ cups water to bowl, fruit purée of choice and food coloring, if using, whisk together. Refrigerate for 2 hours. Pour into ice cream/sorbet maker and follow manufacturer's instructions. Place *nieve* in bowl and fold in add-ins, if using. Freeze for at least 4 hours or up to overnight before serving.

### *Sabores* (Flavorings)

**Coco (*Coconut*):** For flavor: 2 cups coconut purée. For add-in: ½ cup freshly grated coconut. Follow the cooking directions for the base and freeze according to the master recipe.

**Mango (*Mango*):** For flavor: 2 cups mango purée, ½ teaspoon fresh lime juice. Follow the cooking directions for the base and freeze according to the master recipe.

**Mamey (*Mamey Sapote*):** For base: increase to 4 cups sugar and ½ cup corn syrup and cook as specified above. For flavor: 1 large mamey sapote or 4 cups pulp. Place pulp plus 4 cups water in blender and purée into a smooth consistency. Freeze according to the master recipe.

# Nieve de jamaica
## Hibiscus Tea Sorbet | *Makes 1½ quarts*

The unfrozen bases of the following two recipes are commonly served as *aguas frescas*, but both can easily become a delicious frozen dessert, such as a *raspado* or *nieve*. *Flor de jamaica* is dried hibiscus flowers sold in health food stores or Mexican grocery stores as well as farmers markets.

> 2 cups *flor de jamaica* (dried hibiscus flowers)
> 2¾ cups granulated sugar, divided
> ¼ cup light corn syrup

Combine *flor de jamaica*, ¾ cup sugar and 4 cups water in saucepan and place over high heat. Bring to a boil. Reduce to medium heat and allow liquid to reduce by ¼ of its amount, about 10 minutes. Remove from heat and strain into bowl. Discard flowers. Place over ice bath and cool completely.

In another saucepan, combine remaining sugar, corn syrup and 2 cups water. The mixture should resemble wet sand. Place over high heat and bring to a boil. Continue boiling until mixture reaches syrup consistency, about 10 minutes. Add syrup to tea plus 1 cup water, stir to combine. Refrigerate 2 hours. Transfer mixture to an ice cream/ sorbet maker and follow manufacturer's instructions. Freeze for at least 4 hours or up to overnight before serving.

# Nieve de lima
## Lime Sorbet | *Makes 1 quart*

This refreshing sorbet is one of the popular choices at the markets. The lime taste is the perfect thirst-quencher and gives a refreshing element, which are both extremely important during the hot summer months. The essential oils found in the lime zest are the secret to this sorbet's intense flavor. However, do not zest too far into the white pith as this will release a bitter flavor.

> 7 tbsp lime zest
> 1¼ cups granulated sugar
> 2 tbsp fresh lime juice
> 1 drop green food coloring, optional

Place zest plus 4 cups water in a bowl. Allow it to rest for 15 minutes, stirring occasionally. The oils and flavor of zest will intensify. Add sugar and lime juice, stir. Strain. Add food coloring, if using. Transfer mixture to an ice cream/sorbet maker and follow manufacturer's directions. Freeze for 4 hours or up to overnight before serving.

Pictured on the previous two pages (clockwise: *nieve de jamaica*, *nieve de lima*, *nieve de mamey (center)*, *nieve de mango* and *helado de chocolate*)

# Gaznates

## Pastries *with* Meringue Filling | *Makes 16 pieces*

The name of these popular street pastries alludes to its windpipe, or *gaznate*, shape. These deep-fried crunchy "windpipes" are filled with fluffy, pink Italian meringue. They are making them a must-eat when walking through the streets in Mexico. In this recipe, I used two pieces of special equipment: a pasta-maker to roll the dough paper-thin and *cannoli* molds to wrap the dough to acquire the *gaznate* shape. However, you can roll the dough to ⅛ inch in thickness and create your own molds by using sheets of aluminum foil and shaping them into pipes of 1¾ inches in diameter by 6½ inches in length.

For *gaznates*:
- 1⅓ cups all-purpose flour
- ¼ tsp cream of tartar
- 5 eggs, separated
- 2 tbsp granulated sugar
- 1½ tbsp *tequila* silver
- 1½ tsp vanilla extract
- 10 to 12 cups corn oil for deep-frying

For Italian meringue:
- 1 cup granulated sugar
- ⅛ tsp cream of tartar
- 2 drops red food coloring, optional
- ⅛ tsp vanilla extract

Before serving:
- 1 recipe *café de olla* (page 228), optional to accompany

**For *gaznates*:** Combine flour and cream of tartar in bowl and set aside. In a separate bowl, place egg yolks and sugar, whisk until pale. Add *tequila* and vanilla, whisk to combine. Add to flour mixture and knead until dough forms, about 2 minutes. Divide dough into quarters, or into eighths for more manageable sheets, and cover with plastic wrap. Working in batches, flatten one quarter of the dough and pass it through a pasta-maker, slowing increasing the setting to acquire a long paper-thin dough sheet. Cut into four rectangles, about 4-inches by 4-inches in dimension. Lightly spray *cannoli* molds with unflavored cooking spray. Wrap dough in a single layer around the mold, cutting off the excess and dabbing a small amount of water to secure ends.

Pour oil into a Dutch oven or electric fryer, preheat to 350°F. Working two at a time, drop each *gaznate* in the hot oil and fry until golden-brown, about 2 minutes. Place cooked *gaznates* on paper towels to drain. Cool completely before removing the molds or aluminum foil. Set aside until ready to fill.

**For Italian meringue:** Combine ¼ cup water with sugar in a small saucepan. The mixture should resemble wet sand. Place pan over high heat and bring to a boil. Continue boiling until the mixture reaches soft-ball stage, or 240°F on a thermometer, about 10 minutes. Pour reserved egg whites into a mixer fitted with whisk attachment and whisk on low speed until foamy. Add cream of tartar, increase speed until egg whites reach soft peaks, about 6 minutes. Lower speed to low and slowly add sugar in a steady stream. Increase speed to high and continue whisking until meringue has cooled and reached stiff peaks, about 20 minutes. Add food coloring, if using, and vanilla and whisk for 1 minute. Transfer to a pastry bag with a tip.

**Before serving:** Working one at a time, pipe meringue on one side of each *gaznate* and repeat on the other side. Place filled *gaznates* on a platter and accompany with *café de olla*.

# Cuernitos rellenos
## Mexican Cornucopias Filled *with* Pastry Cream | *Makes 8 pieces*

These *cuernitos rellenos* are one of the classic Mexican street sweets. In trying to find a way to recreate this tasty treat from my childhood, I found that thanks to the availability of puff pastry sheets in local supermarkets, *cuernitos rellenos* are extremely easy to make at home. Another important element for this recipe is the cream molds, which are small stainless steel cones found in kitchen supply or specialty baking equipment stores.

**For filling:**

| | |
|---|---|
| 2 **cups whole milk** | ½ **tsp kosher salt** |
| ¾ **cup granulated sugar, divided** | 4 **tbsp cornstarch** |
| 4 **egg yolks** | 2 **tsp vanilla extract** |

**To assemble:**

¼ **cup granulated sugar or as needed**
1 **(9 ½-inch by 9 ½-inch) puff**
  **pastry sheet, thawed according to package directions**
**Powdered sugar as garnish**

**For filling (make ahead up to 3 days):** Combine milk and half the amount of sugar in a medium saucepan and place over medium heat. Stir to combine ingredients, making sure sugar does not stay at the bottom of pan. Bring to a boil, about 10 minutes. Remove from heat. In a separate bowl, whisk together yolks, salt, cornstarch and remaining sugar until thick and pale. Temper yolks by slowing whisking in ½ cup hot cream-milk mixture. Gradually add remaining mixture in a steady stream into yolks, whisking vigorously. Return the egg yolk mixture or custard to a clean saucepan and place over medium heat. Continue cooking until it thickens, whisking continuously, about 3 to 5 minutes. Remove from heat, stir in vanilla and transfer to a bowl. Place over an ice bath to cool. Place plastic wrap directly on the custard to prevent a skin from forming as it cools. Once cool, transfer to a pastry bag and refrigerate until ready to use.

**To assemble:** Preheat oven to 350°F. Place sugar on a small plate and set aside until ready to use.

Place puff pastry on a clean cutting board. Cut into 16 equal strips. Lightly coat cream molds with a light layer of unflavored cooking spray. Working one at a time, brush one side of each puff pastry strip with water; this will be the side touching the mold. Starting at the tip of the cream mold, slowly wrap the puff pastry strip onto the mold, overlapping the edges as it spirals to the top. Two puff pastry strips will be needed for each mold. Lightly brush water on the *cuernito* and roll in the sugar. Place raw *cuernitos* on a sheet pan lined with parchment paper. If re-using molds, place puff pastry strips in the refrigerator until ready to use.

Place *cuernitos* in the oven on middle oven rack and bake until golden brown, about 20 minutes. Remove from oven and set aside to cool slightly. Remove molds. Pipe about ¼ cup of pastry cream into each *cuernito*. Sprinkle with powdered sugar before serving.

Paletas de mango

Paletas de frambuesa

Paletas de rompope

# Paletas de hielo de rompope
### Eggnog Ice Pops | *Makes 8 ice pops*

*Rompope* is a traditional Mexican alcoholic beverage that originated from behind convent walls in Puebla, where this drink was prepared in honor of important visitors. As children, we used to hear about the expert of *rompope* — a nun, who had just taken her vows who always added a secret ingredient. Even though *rompope* has been commercialized and is distributed internationally, some believe that there's still one ingredient that nobody knows. Here is my interpretation of the secret recipe frozen into a delicious ice pop.

**For base:**

| | |
|---|---|
| 2 cups whole milk | ½ tsp vanilla extract |
| ¾ cup granulated sugar | 1 tsp dark rum, optional |
| 1 cinnamon stick | 2 drops yellow food coloring, |
| 3 egg yolks | optional |
| 1¼ cups heavy cream | |

Combine milk, sugar and cinnamon stick in a medium saucepan and place pan over medium heat. Stir to combine ingredients, making sure sugar does not stay at the bottom of the pan. Bring to a boil, about 10 minutes. Remove from heat and steep for 15 minutes to infuse flavors.

Beat egg yolks in a large mixing bowl. Temper yolks by slowly whisking in ½ cup of hot liquid in a steady stream. Gradually add remaining mixture in a steady stream into yolks, whisking vigorously. Return the egg yolk mixture to pan and place over medium heat. Continue cooking until it coats the back of spoon, about 3 minutes, stirring constantly. Strain into bowl and cool completely over an ice bath, about 10 minutes, stirring constantly. Add heavy cream, vanilla, rum and food coloring, if using.

Pour cooled base mixture into 8 ice pop molds and place in freezer for 1 hour to set. Place wooden sticks in center of each mold and freeze until fully set.

.........................................................................................................................

**Variation: *Paletas de hielo de mango*** (Mango Ice Pops) For base: 1 cup granulated sugar, 2 cups mango purée. Place sugar and 2 cups water in saucepan, whisk to combine, and place pan over medium to high heat. Bring to a boil and continue boiling for 5 minutes. Add mango purée, whisk 1 minute and immediately remove from heat. Transfer to bowl, cool to room temperature over an ice water bath. Follow the freezing directions as in recipe above.

**Variation: *Paletas de hielo de frambuesa*** (Raspberry Ice Pops) For base: 1 cup granulated sugar, 4 pints fresh raspberries, 1 tablespoon fresh lime juice. Place sugar and 3 cups water in saucepan and place over medium heat. Bring to a boil, about 4 minutes. Stir in raspberries and lower heat to medium. Cook 3 minutes, add lime juice. Remove from heat, strain and discard pulp. Follow the remaining cooling and freezing directions as in recipe above.

Mazapanes

Palanquetas

*Pepitorias*

*Dulce de coco*

*Garapiñados*
*(with & without food coloring)*

# Dulce de coco
## Coconut Bars | *Makes 24 pieces*

*Cocadas, garapiñados, palanquetas, mazapanes* and *camotes poblanos* are just a few of the many delectable candies made in Puebla. It is said that nuns from the Colonial period in Mexico would distribute their homemade sweets to the townspeople, and as time passed, these *dulces* began to appear in local shops and candy stands — and now in the following recipes. Many can be found in *la calle de los dulces*, or "candies street," located in *6 poniente* between the streets of *5 de Mayo y 4 norte* in Puebla, home to these sweets and more. For the following recipe, use freshly grated coconut, available in the spice aisle or frozen section in selective Mexican grocery stores. Do not confuse with the sweetened coconut found in bags in the baking aisle of the supermarket.

1  (14 oz) can sweetened
    condensed milk
1  (12 oz) can evaporated milk

2½  cups granulated sugar
3¾  cups freshly grated coconut

Place a sheet of parchment paper on a half-sheet pan and lightly coat with non-stick cooking spray or use a silicone pad. Set aside. Combine milks, sugar and coconut in a large saucepan over low to medium heat. Cook mixture until you can see the bottom of the pan and has acquired a light caramel color, about 40 minutes, stirring constantly. Remove from heat and transfer to prepared sheet pan, forming an 8-inch by 9-inch rectangle. Cool completely, about 30 minutes.

Transfer to a cutting board and cut into 1-inch by 3-inches bars. Place on platter or wrap in different colored cellophane paper to give as gifts or after-dinner favors.

# Garapiñados
## Crunchy Candied Peanuts | *Makes 4 cups*

*Garapiñados* are sold in long, cellophane tubes and characterized by their crunchy, sugary texture as well as their bright red color. For this recipe and the next, place peanuts in a single layer on a sheet pan and roast in a 325°F oven for 10 minutes to heighten flavor. Immediately transfer to a separate sheet pan to stop cooking process. Cool completely before proceeding with the recipe.

2  cups unsalted peanuts, roasted as mentioned above
2  cups granulated sugar
1  tsp red food coloring, optional

Combine sugar and 1 cup water in a large saucepan. The mixture should resemble wet sand. Place pan over high heat and bring to a boil. Continue boiling until mixture reaches a thick syrup consistency, about 6 minutes.

Add peanuts and food coloring, if using. Remove from heat and begin stirring constantly. The sugar will break and resemble sand. Return pan to medium heat, stirring constantly until sugar melts once more, about 2 minutes. Transfer to a parchment-lined sheet pan and allow *garapiñados* to dry out at room temperature in a single layer. Serve in a candy bowl or in small bags as gifts.

# Palanquetas de cacahuate
## Mexican Peanut Brittle | *Makes 4 pieces*

*Palanquetas* are commonly seen in rectangular or diamond shape and wrapped in cellophane paper in Mexican candy stands and shops. Their crunchy texture and sweet taste create as much temptation for adults as they do for children. Wrap in different colored cellophane paper to give as fun party favors.

> 1½ cups unsalted peanuts, roasted according to page 216
> 1½ cups granulated sugar
> 1  tsp fresh lime juice

Place a sheet of parchment paper on a half-sheet pan and lightly coat with non-stick cooking spray or use a silicone pad. Set aside. Combine sugar with ¾ cup water in a large saucepan and place over high heat. Bring to a boil. Continue boiling until sugar dissolves and liquid reduces, about 5 minutes. Add peanuts. Once sugar starts to bubble, about 2 minutes, constantly stir with a wooden spoon for 3 minutes more. Remove from heat. Continue to stir until sugar breaks and resembles sand. Add lime juice, return pan over medium heat. Stir for 3 minutes, sugar will begin to melt. Remove from heat and continue to stir for 7 minutes more.

Transfer to sheet pan and using the back of spoon, shape brittle into an 8-inch by 4-inch rectangle. Cool in a dry place for 20 minutes. Using a serrated knife, cut into 4 large rectangles, about 2-inches by 4-inches. Wrap *palanquetas* in cellophane paper.

......................................................................................................

**Variation: *Pepitorias*** (Pumpkin Seed Brittle) Substitute 1 ¼ cups hulled, pumpkin seeds, roasted according to page 216. Follow the rest of the cooking directions as specified above. After adding lime juice, return pan to medium heat, stir for 4 minutes instead of 3 minutes. Cut into six rectangles.

# Mazapanes
## Peanut Confections | *Makes 12 pieces*

These powdery peanut treats are a staple Mexican candy. This recipe took many attempts to recreate both the flavor and most importantly the crumbling effect that distinguishes the *mazapán*. When I finally achieved it, I learned that the secret was in the method of adding the sugar to the paste.

> 1  cup unsalted peanuts, roasted according to page 216
> 1  cup powdered sugar, sifted

Place peanuts in a food processor and process into a smooth paste, about 1 to 2 minutes. Transfer to a mixing bowl. Add sugar in three increments. Using your hands, combine paste with sugar, running your fingers through the mixture to break up any large lumps. The mixture will have a coarse texture.

Place a parchment paper on a sheet pan. Working one at a time, place 3 tablespoons crumbles into a 2-inch round cookie cutter and compact it in. Wrap in 2-inch by 2-inch parchment or cellophane squares and tie with different colored strings to give as a party favor or special treat.

# Camotes Poblanos
## Sweet Potato Candied Rolls | *Makes 20 pieces*

*Camotes poblanos* are characterized by their sugary and crunchy crust and soft interior. The crust is said to be accomplished by sun-drying the candies for several hours. *Camotes poblanos* come in different flavors and colors, such as strawberry, pineapple and more. Here is my interpretation of this classic candy.

- 2 lbs sweet potatoes, peeled, coarsely chopped
- 4½ cups granulated sugar, divided plus more as needed
- ¼ cup canned crushed pineapple, drained

Place a sheet of parchment paper on a half-sheet pan and lightly coat with non-stick cooking spray or use a silicone pad. Set aside. Place sweet potatoes in pot with enough water to cover. Place pot over high heat and bring to a boil. Continue boiling until softened, about 30 to 40 minutes. Strain and mash potatoes into a smooth purée, then set aside

Combine 3½ cups sugar with ¾ cup water in a large saucepan. The mixture should resemble wet sand. Place pan over medium heat and cook until mixture reaches a syrup consistency, about 20 minutes, without stirring. Add purée and pineapple. Continue to stir until it turns into a chewy paste, about 20 minutes. Transfer to sheet pan. Cool enough to handle. Place remaining sugar in a shallow plate.

Divide cooled paste evenly into 20 small rounds. Working one a time, place each round into the sugar and roll into a cylinder about 4 inches long. Transfer sugared rolls to the prepared sheet pan. Roll *camotes* a second time in the sugar and return to sheet pan. Place in the sun or a dry place for 1 hour to dry. Wrap *camotes* with different colored wax paper, twisting ends and tying with colorful pieces of string.

**Note:** For humid climates, turn on oven to 180°F and place sheet pan in oven. The warmth will help dry the *camotes*, allowing the crispy sugar shell to form. Cool completely before wrapping.

# Camotes al vapor
## Steamed Sweet Potatoes *with* Condensed Milk | *Makes 4 pieces*

One thing I strongly believe is that the best street food is found at night — and on wheels. Both my brother Hugo and I remember *el carrito de los camotes* or sweet potato cart, a nomadic steamer with a chimney attached to it. I distinctly remember that no matter the distance, we could hear *el carrito de los camotes* coming as we heard the cart's steam whistle blowing from afar.

- 4 large sweet potatoes, rinsed, cleaned
- Condensed milk as needed

Wrap sweet potatoes in aluminum foil and place in a steamer until fork tender, about 4 hours. Another method to use is to wrap the sweet potatoes in aluminum foil, pierce several holes using a sharp knife and place on a sheet pan in a 375°F oven until fork tender, about 2 hours. Slice in half and drizzle with condensed milk. Enjoy!

# Raspados de guayaba
## Guava Snow Cones | *Makes 6 servings*

*Raspados* were a big part of our childhood because our aunt Petra used to sell them outside the house. She would start the day by making syrups for the snow cones, *flan* and *gelatinas*, or different flavored gelatins, to sell. The following two *raspados* are classic Mexican flavors. *Guayaba,* or guava, is a round, yellow fruit native to Mexico, Central America and South America. They are sweet or sour, depending on their ripeness, with an interior similar to that of a fig and are available in the produce section in Mexican grocery stores or farmers markets. *Raspado de tamarindo* is a special flavor to our family because it was my uncle's favorite remedy to cure a cold — even though it never actually worked, it was delicious! Tamarind pods can be very acidic. Adjust the sugar amount depending on taste.

- 1½ cups granulated sugar
- 12 medium ripe *guayabas* (guavas), washed, coarsely chopped
- 2 drops yellow food coloring, optional
- 3 *guayabas*, sliced, to add to liquid

Place sugar plus 5 cups water in saucepan over medium to high heat and stir to combine. Add the chopped *guayabas*, bring to a boil. Reduce heat and continue to cook until mixture reaches a thick syrup consistency, about 25 minutes. Occasionally stir and stab fruit with spoon to release more flavor. Remove from heat, strain, discard guavas and reserve the liquid. Return liquid to heat and cook 5 minutes more. Add food coloring, if using. Place guava slices in syrup without stirring. Bring back to a boil, about 3 minutes. Continue boiling for 5 more minutes.

Remove from heat and cool completely, about 1 hour. Working one serving at a time, put 2 cups ice in blender and crush to a grainy consistency. Transfer to plastic cup and drizzle over 5 to 6 tablespoons syrup. Top with whole guava slices and serve.

.................................................................................................

**Variation:** ***Raspados de tamarindo*** (Tamarind Snow Cones) Substitute 16 tamarind pods for chopped and sliced *guayabas*. Reserve a few cooked tamarind pods for garnish when straining liquid. Omit food coloring. Follow the rest of the cooking and ice crushing directions as specified above. Reduce amount of syrup to 3 to 4 tablespoons per serving. Garnish and serve.

Bebidas

**Bebidas** are drinks that can range from refreshing Mexican *aguas frescas*, hot *atoles*, and nutritious *licuados* to strong *tepache*. The most common ones seen in the streets are *aguas frescas*. They can be either fruit-based, blending your favorite type of fruit and adding a small amount of sugar, or they can require some type of cooking method or soaking, as seen in the recipes for the three most traditional *aguas* on page 235: *horchata*, *tamarindo* or *jamaica*. A*guas frescas* are sold at drink stands throughout Mexico's city streets. Very popular during the hot summer months, they are showcased in large, beautiful glass jars and sold in plastic bags tied with rubber bands that secure the liquid inside and support a straw. During the winter months, hot drinks, such as *atoles* (page 232), *champurrado* (page 231) and *chocolate caliente* (page 231) are more commonly sold at the *mercados*.

Like many of the street foods featured throughout this book, Mexican beverages take time, specially selected ingredients and traditional equipment to make. Hot drinks are made in earthenware pots — *ollas* or *cazuelas*. Some require a *molinillo*, or a wooden whisk, that is placed in between the palms of the hands and twisted constantly to aerate the drink as it warms up. These hot drinks are the usual accompaniments for sweet pastries like *cuernitos rellenos*, *tamales de dulces* or *churros*.

*Atoles* require *masa* as a thickening agent and constant stirring to prevent the milk from boiling over and burning. Use *masa para tamales*, mentioned on page 248, to give the best taste for these drinks. For *horchata* (page 235), it is customary to leave the rice soaking overnight, then take it to the local mill and have it ground up into a paste to use as base for the drink. Such a *molino*, or mill, exists in the local *mercado* in Mérida, Yucatán. The vendors at *Casa Molinos* pass the rice through the mill, pour water infused with cinnamon, which add an extra level of flavor, and turn the rice into a base. People take the base home and add water or milk to flavor to their liking.

There is a special drink for every occasion and season. My brother Ruben helped in researching and developing the recipes so we could offer a little bit of everything. Recipes for refreshing drinks for the summer as well as for hot beverages for cold winter days, and a few for in-between, can be found in the following pages. Enjoy!

## Lechero
### Hot Milk *with* Espresso | *Makes 4 servings*

*La Parroquia*, a little coffee shop located in the port of Veracruz, has been an icon when it comes to coffee for more than 200 years. One of their specialties is the *café lechero*, similar to a *café au lait* or a latte, with a twist. The customer receives a shot of espresso in a tall glass. The waiter then comes with a hot mixture of milks in a tea kettle and pours it into the glass holding the kettle so high up, a long stream forms (page 224). Here is my interpretation of this wonderful coffee drink.

| | |
|---|---|
| 3  cups whole milk | 2  tbsp condensed milk |
| 1  cup evaporated milk | 1  cup brewed espresso coffee |

Combine milks in a medium pot and place over medium heat. Bring to a boil, about 10 minutes, stirring occasionally.

Evenly divide espresso among four tall glasses or coffee mugs. Pour 1 cup hot milk mixture onto each glass. Make sure to hold the kettle at a high enough distant when pouring in order to create a little bit of froth in each serving.

## Café de olla
### Traditional Hot Coffee | *Makes 4 servings*

For a good cup of Mexican coffee, the coffee beans are infused with cinnamon and *piloncillo* — unrefined sugar used in Mexican cooking. In this recipe, Mexican *chocolate* and orange zest are both added to elevate the flavors. Both Mexican *chocolate* and *piloncillo* can be purchased in Mexican grocery stores or in the Hispanic/ethnic foods aisle in major supermarkets. If *piloncillo* is unavailable, substitute for equal parts brown sugar.

| | |
|---|---|
| ½  cup good-quality coffee beans | ¼  cup *piloncillo* or brown sugar |
| 4  tsp Mexican *chocolate* | ⅓  cinnamon stick |
| 1  tsp orange zest | |

Coarsely chop coffee beans in a food processor. Do not grind into a fine powder because the coarser the coffee beans, the easier to strain. Transfer to a pot. Add 4 cups water, *chocolate*, orange zest and *piloncillo*. Place pot over high heat. Bring to a boil, about 3 minutes.

Remove from heat and add cinnamon stick. Allow liquid to steep for 15 minutes. Strain, using a fine-mesh sieve. Serve hot.

# Chocolate caliente
## Hot Chocolate | *Makes 4 servings*

The best early morning breakfast on the streets is a nice hot cup of *chocolate caliente* with some *churros*, sweet *tamales* or fresh-baked sweet goods from a bakery. In this particular recipe, water and milk can be used interchangeably. At Hugo's restaurant, we make our own *chocolate criollo* but any brand of Mexican *chocolate* can be used for this recipe.Usually sold in 3-ounce tablets, it is available in Mexican grocery stores or in the Hispanic/ethnic foods aisle in local supermarkets. In this recipe, use a hand blender to create the foam in the *chocolate* before serving. Always use caution when dealing with hot liquid.

> 4  **cups whole milk or water**
> 2  **tablets (3 oz each) Mexican *chocolate*, broken into chunks**

Combine milk or water and *chocolate* in a pot and place over medium heat. Bring to a boil, about 10 minutes. Stir continuously to completely dissolve *chocolate*. Remove from heat. Using a hand blender, mix liquid until foamy, about 2 minutes. Serve hot.

# Champurrado
## Chocolate Porridge | *Makes 4 servings*

*Champurrado* is an *atole* with *chocolate*. This particular hot drink requires *masa* for a thickening agent. Use *masa para tamales*, which can be purchased at select Mexican grocery stores, as well as for Mexican *chocolate*. For this recipe, slightly soften *chocolate* in the microwave for 45 seconds to make it easier to break into chunks.

> ¾  **lb *masa para tamales***
> 2½ **tablets (3 oz each) Mexican *chocolate*, softened**

Combine 4 cups water, *masa* and *chocolate* in a pot and place over medium heat. Bring to a boil, about 8 to 10 minutes. Reduce heat and simmer until it thickens, about 15 minutes. Stir occasionally. Remove from heat. Serve hot.

# Atole de arroz
## Hot Rice Drink *with* Cinnamon | *Makes 6 servings*

*Atole* is a traditional Mexican drink that requires constant stirring to prevent the milk from burning. Growing up, it was a family tradition to prepare *atole* every afternoon, and it fell on us kids to stir. However, I remember on one occasion it was Ruben's turn. I began to smell something burning so I ran into the kitchen and saw Ruben holding the wooden spoon, his eyes closed and head drooping down. The *atole* was burned and had boiled over and was all over the stove. I strongly suggest keeping your eye on the stove while preparing this recipe.

| | |
|---|---|
| ½ cup long grain rice | ¾ cup granulated sugar |
| 1 cinnamon stick | 1 tsp vanilla extract |
| 8 cups whole milk | |

Combine rice and cinnamon stick with ¾ cup water in a pot and place over low heat. Bring to a simmer, and continue simmering for 10 minutes. Remove from heat and tightly cover for 10 minutes.

In a separate saucepan, add milk and place over medium heat. Bring to a simmer, about 7 minutes. Remove from heat. Add hot milk to rice. Return pot to medium heat and bring to a boil, about 3 minutes. Lower heat and add sugar and vanilla, stir to dissolve sugar. Allow mixture to simmer until rice is tender, about 40 minutes, stirring constantly. Remove from heat, cover, and allow it to rest for 15 minutes. Serve warm.

# Atole de mora negra
## Blackberry Masa Drink | *Makes 4 servings*

For this recipe, *masa para tamales* is also used as a thickening agent, similar to the *champurrado* on page 231. Substitute your favorite berry. Adjust sugar to taste.

| | |
|---|---|
| 1 cinnamon stick | 1 pint blackberries, washed |
| ½ cup *masa para tamales* | 6 tbsp granulated sugar |

Combine 4 cups water with cinnamon stick in a pot and place over medium heat. Bring to a boil, about 8 to 10 minutes. Meanwhile, combine *masa*, blackberries and 1 cup water in blender. Purée into a smooth consistency. Strain. Add to hot liquid.

Bring mixture back to a boil, about 4 minutes. Reduce heat and add sugar, stir. Simmer mixture until it thickens, about 8 to 12 minutes. Stir constantly. Remove from heat. Serve warm.

# Horchata
### Rice *and* Milk Drink | *Makes 6-8 servings*

The following three recipes are the most traditional *aguas frescas* found in Mexican drink stands. The recipe for *horchata* can be made in a variety of ways. Some leave the rice soaking over night and others toast the rice before pulverizing it. I found that both ways work well but I preferred the taste and quickness from the toasted-pulverized version.

| | |
|---|---|
| 1 cup uncooked long grain rice | 2 cups whole milk |
| 1 cinnamon stick, broken in pieces | 3 tsp vanilla extract |
| | 1 cup granulated sugar |

Place sauté pan over medium heat, preheat 1 minute. Add rice and cinnamon. Toast 2 minutes, stirring constantly to prevent rice from burning. Remove from heat. Transfer to a sheet pan to cool. Place in spice grinder or blender. Pulverize into a fine powder. Transfer powder to a mixing bowl and add 6 cups water and milk, stir to combine. Add vanilla and sugar, stir. Using fine-mesh sieve, strain into a pitcher. Serve in glasses with ice.

# Agua de tamarindo
### Tamarind Drink | *Makes 4 servings*

Some tamarind pods are more acidic than others. Adjust sugar to taste. It is very important to leave the tamarind pods in the liquid as it cools to fully infuse and concentrate the flavor into the *agua fresca*. If desired, you may blend some of the pods with the liquid to add more body to the drink.

14 tamarind pods
1 cup granulated sugar

Bring 4 cups water to a rolling boil. Add pods and return to a boil, about 2 minutes. The water will begin to turn to a dark caramel color. Add sugar. Reduce heat and leave gently bubbling for 5 minutes more. Remove from heat. Allow it to steep for 2 hours. Strain. Using the back of a wooden spoon, smash the pods against the colander to extract all the juices as you strain the liquid. If desired, purée a few of the smashed pods in blender with ½ cup liquid, return purée to pitcher, stir, and discard the remaining pods. Serve chilled in glasses with ice.

# Agua de jamaica
### Hibiscus Tea | *Makes 4 servings*

This dark, cranberry-colored drink is a refreshing herbal tea. Some street vendors add red food coloring to intensify the color even more. Dried hibiscus flowers, or *flor de jamaica*, are available in health food stores or Mexican grocery stores.

1 cup *flor de jamaica* (dried hibiscus flowers)
⅓ cup granulated sugar

Place *flor de jamaica* in a fine-mesh sieve and rinse briefly with cold, running water. This helps revive the flower's vibrant red color. Transfer to a saucepan and add 2 cups water. Place over high heat and bring to a rolling boil. Immediately remove from heat. Cool completely. Strain into pitcher and discard flowers. Add sugar and 2 cups more water to pitcher, stir. Serve chilled in glasses with ice.

# Licuado de plátano
## Banana Smoothie | *Makes 4 servings*

*Licuados* or smoothies are common breakfast items sold at the many *tianguis*. They are made with your choice of fruit, milk and sweetened with a small amount of sugar. Sometimes uncooked rolled oats will be added to increase the nutrition and fiber content.

| | |
|---|---|
| 4 ripe bananas, peeled, sliced | 1½ tbsp granulated sugar |
| 2 cups whole milk | Ground cinnamon for garnish |
| ½ tsp vanilla extract | |

Place bananas, milk, vanilla and sugar in blender. Blend into a smooth, velvety consistency, about 1 minute. Serve in tall glasses. Garnish with a sprinkle of cinnamon.

......................................................................................................................

**Variation:** *Licuado de fresa* (Strawberry Smoothie) Substitute 2 cups washed, sliced strawberries, 3 ½ cups whole milk, 5 tablespoons granulated sugar, 1 teaspoon vanilla extract and 1 cup ice. Follow the blending procedure as specified above.

# Licuado de mamey
## Mamey Sapote Smoothie | *Makes 4 servings*

This particular *licuado* is one of my favorites due to the *mamey* fruit's unique flavor. *Mamey* is native to southern Mexico and Central America. It has a brown, fuzzy exterior and a salmon-pink and orange interior. Its buttery texture is similar to a cooked sweet potato. *Mamey* is common for *licuados*, ice creams and sorbets as seen on page 204. *Mamey* can be found in the produce section of Mexican grocery stores and farmers markets. It is worth seeking out a source for this delicious fruit.

| | |
|---|---|
| 1 medium mamey sapote, peeled, pitted | 4 cups whole milk |
| 1 cup ice | 1 tsp vanilla extract |
| 3 tbsp granulated sugar | Ground cinnamon for garnish |

Place pulp, ice, sugar, milk and vanilla in blender. Blend into a smooth, velvety consistency, about 1 minute. Serve in tall glasses. Garnish with a sprinkle of cinnamon.

......................................................................................................................

**Variation:** *Licuado de mango* (Mango Smoothie) Substitute 2 ripe mangoes, 3 cups whole milk, ¼ cup granulated sugar, 1 teaspoon vanilla extract and 1 cup ice. Follow the blending directions as specified above.

# Agua de sandía
## Watermelon Drink | *Makes 4 servings*

The following a*guas frescas* are very easy to make. Accompany with spicy roasted peanuts, recipe offered below. This combination is great at outdoor parties. For the following recipe, buy a 3-pound watermelon and use ¼ of it for the *agua fresca*, cube the rest and toss with lime juice and Mexican chili powder and offer as a snack — a popular way to buy fruit on Mexican streets. Serve these drinks in glasses with ice. Do not place ice in the pitcher as this will water down the flavor.

| | |
|---|---|
| ¼ **(3 lb) watermelon, flesh only, cut into 1-inch cubes** | 1 **cup granulated sugar**<br>2 **tsp fresh lime juice** |

Place watermelon, sugar and 1 ½ cups water in blender. Blend into a smooth consistency, about 2 minutes. Pour into a mesh strainer placed over a large bowl. Push pulp against sides of the sieve to squeeze out as much of the liquid as possible. Discard pulp. Transfer to pitcher, add lime juice, and stir. Serve in glasses with ice.

. . . . . . . . . . . . . . . . . . . . . . . . . . . . . . . . . . . . . . . . . . . . . . . . . . . . . . . . . . . . . . . . . . . . . . . . . . . . . . . . .

**Variation: *Agua de piña*** (Pineapple) Substitute 1 (3 lb) ripe pineapple, peeled, cut into 1-inch cubes, ¾ cup sugar. Follow the blending, straining, and serving procedure as specified above. Omit the lime juice.

**Variation: *Agua de melón*** (Cantaloupe) Substitute 1 (2 ½ lb) cantaloupe, peeled, seeded, cut into 1-inch cubes, 2 cups granulated sugar, ½ teaspoon fresh lime juice. Follow the blending instructions using 2 cups water. Strain and serve as specified above.

**Variation: *Agua de lima*** (Lime) Substitute ½ cup fresh lime juice, 1 tablespoon lime zest, ½ cup plus 1 tablespoon granulated sugar. Combine 3 cups water, lime juice and zest in a bowl. Steep 5 minutes. Strain into a pitcher. Add sugar and ½ cup more water. Stir. Serve as specified above.

# Cacahuates en vaso
## Spicy Roasted Peanuts | *Makes 2 cups*

This popular Mexican snack is sold in plastic cups at street stands. Peanuts are slow roasted, tossed in lime juice and chili powder. *Cacahuates en vaso* are very spicy but you can't eat just a few. I recommend a cold *agua fresca* standing nearby.

| | |
|---|---|
| 1 **tsp cayenne pepper**<br>1 **tsp paprika**<br>½ **tsp kosher salt** | 2 **cups peanuts, hulled,**<br>**raw, unsalted**<br>¼ **cup fresh lime juice** |

Preheat oven to 200°F. In bowl, combine cayenne pepper, paprika and salt. Set aside.

Place peanuts in a sheet pan in a single layer and place in oven. Roast for 40 to 45 minutes. Remove from oven and transfer to another sheet pan. Cool completely. Transfer to a bowl. Add lime juice and toss. Sprinkle spice mixture and toss once again. Transfer to a sheet pan and return to warm oven to dry for 2 hours. Remove from oven and cool completely before serving. Serve in small bowls at parties.

# Agua de piña con nopal
## Pineapple *and* Cactus Drink | *Makes 4-6 servings*

The amazing thing about *aguas frescas* is that you can combine any fruit in any way and create a refreshing drink. In this recipe, I combine a fresh, ripe pineapple and *nopal*, or cactus paddle. In any of the other *agua frescas*, feel free to use your favorite fruits alone or together. Also, the fruit from the *nopal* — the prickly pear or *tuna* — is also a great fruit for an *agua fresca*, as seen below.

| | |
|---|---|
| ½ (3 lb) ripe pineapple, peeled, cut into chunks | ½ large Granny Smith apple with skin, cored |
| 1 small *nopal* (cactus paddle), cleaned, coarsely chopped | ½ cup granulated sugar |

Place pineapple, cactus paddle, apple and 5 cups water in blender. Blend into a smooth consistency, about 2 minutes. Strain into a pitcher. Add sugar, stir. Serve in glasses with ice.

........................................................................................

**Variation: *Agua de tuna*** (Prickly Pear) Substitute 6 *tunas*, washed, peeled, quartered, 3 tablespoons granulated sugar, 1 ½ teaspoons fresh lime juice. Place *tunas*, sugar, lime juice and 1 cup water in blender. Blend 1 minute. Do not purée too long to prevent cracking all the seeds as this will turn the *agua fresca* black. Strain, if desired, into pitcher, add 1 cup more water, stir. Serve as specified above.

# Tepache
## Fermented Pineapple Drink | *Makes 6 servings*

This recipe calls for the use of the whole pineapple. *Tepache* is the name of a municipality in Sonora, Mexico, as well as a traditional Mexican fermented drink that is infused with pineapple chunks and rind. It is sweetened with *piloncillo*, or unrefined sugar, and uses spices such as cinnamon and whole cloves. For this recipe, I added dark beer and left it fermenting in a dark place in a sealed plastic container.

| | |
|---|---|
| ½ (3 lb) pineapple, crown removed | ¾ cup dark beer |
| | 3 whole cloves |
| ½ cup *piloncillo* or brown sugar | 1 cinnamon stick |

Peel pineapple, reserving rind, and cut into chunks. Place in a re-sealable plastic container. Add to the pineapple: *piloncillo*, dark beer, whole cloves, cinnamon stick and 6 cups water, stir to combine. Tightly cover and place in a dark place for 48 hours to ferment. Use a large wire-mesh strainer to strain fermented mixture into pitcher. Discard pineapple chunks and rind. Adjust sweetness by adding more *piloncillo* or brown sugar to liquid. Add more water in case alcohol flavor is too strong. Serve in chilled glasses or with ice.

# Glossary

**Achiote:** A red seasoning paste that is commonly sold in block form, it is used primarily in marinades and *salsas*. Found in Mexican grocery stores or in the Hispanic/ethnic foods aisle of the supermarket.

**Asiento:** Unrefined pork fat typically used in *antojito* stands in Mexico. Substitute with melted lard.

**Banana leaves:** Large, green aromatic leaves used as wrappings for *tamales* and meats that will be steamed, barbecued or grilled. Found in Mexican/Asian grocery stores or farmers markets.

**Cebollitas cambray:** Mexican green onions with a larger bulb than common green onions. Found in Mexican grocery stores or farmers markets.

**Chiles, dried:** Different types of dried peppers are found in the spice aisle or in the produce section of Mexican grocery stores and selective supermarkets. For proper toasting and reconstituting procedures, refer to page 116.

   **Ancho:** Originated in Puebla, it is a mild, wide dried pepper that comes from drying the fresh *poblano* pepper.

   **Chile de árbol:** A small and thin red dried pepper.

   **Chipotle:** A dried smoked *jalapeño*. Sold simply dried and smoked, they are more commonly used in recipes in their canned form when combined with an adobo sauce.

   **Guajillo:** These 4 inch long by 1 inch wide dried peppers have a burgundy skin and are mild in hotness; they are said to have a green-tea flavor with berry undertones. They have a tougher skin than other dried peppers so might require longer soaking. Produced from drying the fresh *mirasol* pepper.

   **Mulato:** A brownish-black dried pepper of mild to medium heat, it is on average 4 inches long and 2 ½ inches in diameter. Produced from drying the *poblano* pepper like the *ancho* but at a different ripening stage. Ancho chiles are picked when red while *mulato* are allowed to turn a dark brown before drying.

   **Pasilla:** This dried pepper is about 6 inches long by 1 inch wide with dark brown skin and is mild in hotness.

   **Pulla:** An elongated and slightly curved deep red dried pepper with a tapered point. It is about 3 to 4 inches in length. It has a thin flesh and a light fruity flavor with a hint of licorice.

**Chiles, fresh:** Although many of the following peppers can be found in major supermarkets, they are available in Mexican grocery stores as well as farmers markets. For proper roasting and peeling procedures, refer to page 116. Use gloves when removing seeds and veins of the hottest peppers.

**Chilaca:** Similar to *poblano* peppers but thinner, longer and a bit darker, this fresh pepper is mild to medium-hot and can be used whenever a recipe calls for a *poblano* and vice versa. When dried, it is known as *pasilla*.

**Habanero:** Considered one of the hottest peppers in the world, this small and lantern-shaped pepper is common to the Yucatán. It can be light green to bright orange when fully ripe. Wear gloves when handling.

**Jalapeño:** Named after Xalapa (pronounced Jalapa), capital city of Veracruz, where traditionally it is cultivated, this fresh pepper has a smooth dark green skin which becomes red when allowed to fully ripen, and can be hot to extremely hot. They are about 2 inches long and 1 inch in diameter, and seeds and veined can be easily removed. When dried, they are called *chipotles*.

**Poblano:** A dark triangular-shaped green-colored pepper, about 2½ to 3 inches wide and 4 to 5 inches long. The taste is mild and the shape makes it great for *chiles rellenos*.

**Serrano:** Similar to *jalapeños* but with a bit more heat, this small pepper is great for *salsas*. Remove seeds and veins to reduce heat level, if desired.

**Chocolate:** Mexican *chocolate* is sold in 3-oz tablets in the Hispanic/ethnic foods aisle in major supermarkets or Mexican grocery stores. The common brand is *chocolate Abuelita* but any Mexican *chocolate* works well for the recipes in this book.

**Clamato® tomato cocktail juice:** Tomato juice with a blend of spices and a touch of clam broth, this cocktail juice is commonly used to make *cocteles* or seafood cocktails. Clamato® is the most common brand and is found in the juices or cocktail drink mix/liquor aisles in major supermarkets.

**Comal:** This is an essential piece of equipment for Mexican cooking. For a detailed description, refer to page 17.

**Crema Mexicana:** A mild-tasting topping is similar to crème fraîche but runnier in consistency. Found in the refrigerated section of both Mexican grocery stores and selective supermarkets. It is drizzled on *flautas*, *enchiladas* and more. If unavailable, substitute with sour cream, keeping in mind this has a thicker consistency.

**Epazote:** This aromatic and flavorful herb is used in Mexican and Latin-American cuisines and can be purchased in Mexican grocery stores and farmers markets.

**Flores de calabaza:** Squash blossoms, which are available in Mexican farmers markets or selective organic grocery stores, are great to stuff as well as eat in *quesadillas*. Remove stems before using and lightly rinse under water. Allow to fully dry before using.

**Huitlacoche:** This food item has been part of Mexican cuisine since the days of the Aztecs. Native to Mexico, it is a fungus that grows on corn on the cob due to the excess moisture in the atmosphere. Its appear-

ance is extremely ugly and many farms in the United States go to extreme lengths to stop it from occurring in their crops. However, *huitlacoche* is quite delicious and popular as fillings in *quesadillas* and *tacos* throughout street stands in Mexico. Fresh *huitlacoche* is a rare find, but the best choice. Look for it at farm stands when local corn is in season. It is more readily available in canned form or fresh frozen at Mexican grocery stores.

**Lard**: Pork fat used in Mexican cuisine. Substitute equal parts with corn oil, if desired.

**Maggi® jugo sazonador:** This liquid vegetable-based seasoning sauce is used for marinades, soups and sauces and is distributed by Nestlé® all over the world. Manufactured in Mexico under the Maggi® brand name as *Jugo Sazonador*, look for it in Mexican grocery stores.

**Mamey:** *Mamey sapote* is a traditional Mexican fruit. It has a brown, fuzzy exterior, orange and pinkish flesh and has a dark, oval-shaped pit. It is available in the produce section of Mexican grocery stores or farmers markets.

**Masa, fresh:** This Mexican "dough-like" substance is made out corn kernels that have been simmered in slaked lime, hulled and then passed through a mill and ground. For a detailed description and availability, refer to page 24. *Masa* stays fresh in the refrigerator for up to three days.

**Masa harina:** This instant corn *masa* flour mix is available in the Hispanic aisle in major supermarkets that can be used as an alternative to fresh *masa*. It is a powdery substance made out of dried corn kernels that have been simmered in slaked lime,

ground and then allowed to dry into a flour-like substance. Follow the packaged instructions to prepare.

**Masa harina para tamales:** This instant corn *masa* flour mix is similar to the one mentioned above but is designed to be used to make *tamales*, which will be specified on the package. It is available in the Hispanic/ethnic foods aisle in selective major supermarkets and Mexican grocery stores. Follow the packaged instructions to prepare.

**Masa para tamales:** Fresh *masa* with a coarser texture, which makes fluffier *tamales* and allows the corn husk they are steamed in to be peeled off more easily. It is available refrigerated in 5-lb plastic bags in Mexican grocery stores and select Mexican butcher shops. This can also be used as a thickening agent for *atoles*. Adjust consistency by adding 4 tablespoon each lard and chicken stock per 1 pound *masa*; mixing in a stand-up mixer fitted with paddle attachment until light and airy, about 20 minutes; and dropping a dollop of *masa* in a cup of water to test readiness; it must float to top. If not, continue mixing for 1 additional minute. Add salt to taste.

**Mexican chili powder:** This type of chili powder can be found in the Hispanic/ethnic foods aisle in major supermarkets. At Hugo's restaurant, we make our own version by pulverizing 2 toasted *guajillo* peppers and combining that with 1 teaspoon paprika. Use it on fruit or cucumber drenched in lime juice for a quick street food snack.

**Mexican oregano**: This type of oregano is more savory than the typical one used in Italian-American cuisine. It is available in the spice aisle in large supermarkets and

is labeled "Mexican" on the bottle. Crumble before adding to any dish. Yucatecan oregano is five times more flavorful than Mexican oregano, and is available online from mail order sources (page 249).

**Nopales:** Cactus paddles are sold in a variety of ways in Mexican grocery stores. For convenience, the cleaned fleshy pads are sold in bags, sometimes already sliced and cubed. If buying fresh with spines, clean using a sharp knife. Run knife close to flesh and scrape off all spines. Wear gloves when handling. Cook according to instructions on page 183.

**Flor de jamaica:** Dried hibiscus flowers used to make a popular *agua fresca*. It is available in health food stores, Mexican farmers markets as well as the spice aisle in Mexican grocery stores. It is important to remove liquids made with *flor de jamaica* from the heat as soon as they boil; if left longer, the flowers will release a bitter taste. Cool immediately.

**Papalo:** A pungent and aromatic herb with a strong flavor that grows wild throughout parts of Mexico and is frequently used in the cuisine from Puebla. It is available in selective Mexican farmers markets. Cilantro can be used as an alternative, although it is quite different in taste, but will add a fresh touch to the food.

**Piloncillo:** Unrefined Mexican brown sugar. When the sugar canes are crushed, the remaining juice is collected, boiled and poured into molds, which then hardens into blocks. It is available in cone shape in Mexican grocery stores as well as select supermarkets.

**Pipicha:** A pungent herb from Oaxaca, it is used in traditional Mexican cooking, particularly in *salsas* and stews. It looks similar to tarragon leaves and can be purchased in select Mexican farmers markets.

**Pulque:** A milk-colored and somewhat viscous alcoholic beverage, it is made from the fermentation of the *maguey* and *agave* plant. It is rarely available outside of Mexico. Use Mexican beer as a substitute when *pulque* is called for in traditional Mexican recipes.

**Quesos:** Mexican cheeses add unique flavor dimensions to any dish. Many have made their way to the dairy section of major supermarkets. If not, I suggest visiting local Mexican grocery stores to find these treasures. Some of the Mexican cheeses available are:

**Quesillo or queso Oaxaca:** This semi-firm string cheese from Oaxaca is shaped like a ball of yarn and has great melting qualities as well as a mellow taste.

**Queso Chihuahua or Chihuahua cheese:** This soft white cow's milk cheese with good melting qualities is ideal to use in *quesadillas*. It originates from the state of Chihuahua where it is known as *queso menonita*, which alludes to the Mennonite communities where this cheese was originally made.

**Queso Cotija:** This hard cow's milk cheese originated in Cotija, Michoacán. It is a crumbly as well as a bit salty. It is available grated in bags or rounds for you to crumble.

**Queso fresco:** This "fresh cheese" is the most common one used in Mexican cooking, as it goes well with many things: crumbled on top *refritos*, soups, salads, as well for garnish. It has a slight acidic flavor and is sold in rounds.

**Tortilla press:** a special piece of equipment used in *tortilla* making. See page 74 for more information.

**Tomatillo:** This "little tomato" is green with a brownish husk, which must be removed before use. Rinse with cold water as they tend to have a sticky film. It is used mainly for *salsas*. Roast according to instructions on page 116 before using.

**White corn:** Commonly used in Mexican cooking to make *elotes asados*, served in cups and for *esquites*. It can be purchased in the produce section in selective Mexican grocery stores and at farmers markets when in season. If unavailable, yellow corn can be used instead, keeping in mind that it is sweeter than white corn. To properly remove kernels from the cob, use a sharp knife to slice off pointed end of cob to give a stable base. Run knife down the cob to remove kernels, about ¼ inch from the cob. Do not cut too close to the cob to prevent cutting hull that attaches the kernels, which is bitter, tough and unpleasant to eat.

**Hojas de aguacate:** These dried avocado leaves release a mild anise flavor and are very common in Mexican cuisine. They are available in the spice aisle in selective Mexican grocery stores and from mail order sources on page 249.

**Valentina® sauce:** This vinegar-based spicy Mexican chili sauce can be purchased in Mexican grocery stores or in the Hispanic/ethnic foods aisle in major supermarkets.

**Tamarindo:** Tamarind is an acidic and juicy pod greatly used to make *agua fresca*, *raspado* or eaten as a whole. Even though the tamarind pod is indigenous to Africa, it was introduced to Mexico in the 16th century. It is cultivated in the tropical regions of Mexico, such as Michoacán, Guerrero, Oaxaca, Chiapas and even Yucatán.

**Xoconostle:** A sour prickly pear typically used in Mexican cooking for *salsas*, it can be found in selective Mexican farmers markets or in the produce section of Mexican grocery stores.

## Mail Order Sources

**Frieda's Inc.**
**Global Headquarters**
4465 Corporate Center Drive
Los Alamitos, CA 90720-2561
714.826.6100
www.friedas.com

Dried chiles (*ancho, mulato, chipotle, chile de árbol, guajillo, morita, pasilla*)
Fresh peppers *(chilaca, habanero, jalapeño, poblano, serrano)*
Other Mexican ingredients (*epazote,* corn husks, cinnamon sticks, tamarind pods, *tomatillos, piloncillo*)

**Herbs of Mexico**
3903 Whitter Boulevard
Los Angeles, CA 90023
323.261-2521
www.herbsofmexico.com

Pumpkin seeds (*pepitas)*, Mexican oregano, cinnamon sticks, cumin seeds, dried hibiscus flowers

**MexGrocer.com**
4060 Morena Blvd., Suite C
San Diego, CA 92117
877.463.9476
www.mexcroger.com

Mexican equipment (*comal, tamalera, molcajete, tortilla* press)
Mexican ingredients (*masa harina*, Mexican *chocolate*, chipotle in adobo, *crema Mexicana*, banana leaves, *achiote* paste, Mexican vanilla extract, Maggi® brand *jugo sazonador)*
Mexican cheeses (*quesillo* also known as *queso Oaxaca, queso fresco, cotija*)

**GourmetSleuth, Inc.**
P.O. Box 508
Los Gatos, CA 95031
408.354.8281
www.gourmetsleuth.com

Dried avocado leaves, banana leaves, dried shrimp, dried chile peppers and in powdered form (*ancho, mulato, guajillo, chile de árbol)*
Mexican *chocolate*-making kit (*cazuela* and *molinillo)*, blue corn *masa*, dried corn kernels, *cal* (slaked lime)

**Melissa Guerra**
**At Pearl Brewery in the**
**Full Goods Bldg.**
200 East Grayson, Suite 122
San Antonio, TX 78215
210.293.3983
www.melissaguerra.com

Dried chile peppers (*ancho, chipotle, guajillo, pulla, morita, mulato)*
Mexican ingredients (*masa harina*, corn husks, dried corn for *masa*, Mexican *chocolate* and coffee, *piloncillo*, dried hibiscus flowers)
Mexican artisanal items

**Penzeys Spices**
*Retail Store and online*
Houston, TX
516 W 19th Street
713.862.6777
www.penzeys.com

Dried peppers (*ancho, chile de árbol, guajillo, chipotle)*
Other items (*jalapeño* peppers, cinnamon sticks, *epazote*, Mexican oregano)

**Pendery's**
*Retail store and online*
1407 8th Avenue
Ft. Worth, TX 76104
817.924.3434
www.penderys.com

Dried peppers (*ancho, chile de árbol, guajillo, mulato)*
Other items (cinnamon sticks, dried hibiscus flowers, *tortilla* press, corn husks)

**La Vaquita Products**
Castro Cheese Co., Inc
4006 Campbell Road
Houston, TX 77080
713.460.0329
www.castrocheese.com

Mexican cheeses (*cotija, queso fresco, quesillo* also known as *queso Oaxaca)*
Mexican dairy products such as *crema Mexicana*

## Houston Sources

**Canino Produce Co.**
**Houston's Farmers Market**
2520 Airline Dr.
Houston, TX 77009
713.862.4027
www.caninoproduce.com

**Fiesta Mart**
*Although there are 50 locations throughout Houston, Austin, Dallas/Ft. Worth areas, these are the ones I visit most for Mexican ingredients. Visit www.fiestamart. com for a location near you.*

12355 Main
Houston, TX 77035
713.551.7575

2300 N. Shepherd Drive
Houston, TX 77008
713.869.6188

**La Michoacana Meat Market**
*There are more than 100 locations throughout Texas, mainly distributed in the east. Visit www. lamichoacanameatmarket.com for a location nearest you.*

1220 1960 FM W. Rd.
Houston, TX, 77090
281.440.0551

1348 N. Shepherd
Houston, TX, 77008
713.862.6129

**Central Market**
3815 Westheimer
Houston, TX 77027
713.386.1700

**H-E-B**
*For overall ingredients, visit your nearby H-E-B stores, which have a selective variety of international foods.*

1701 W. Alabama Street
Houston, TX 77098
Corporate #630
713.529.2474

# Acknowledgements

Ruben and I want to thank those who helped us in the preparation of this book. First of all, special thanks to Cristina Ramírez Vargas who worked alongside us as we tested and retested recipes and made sure our vision was on-track throughout the book. Julia Pemberton Hellums advised us on the form of the book as its editor. Her wisdom and attention to detail, both in cooking techniques and in what it takes to create a book, were key to this project. She patiently guided us through the process, helped us break up the project into manageable bits and kept us on deadline. If you know Ruben and I, that was quite an accomplishment. We were so impressed by Wyn Bomar's layout and her artistic touches. We loved her sensitivity to the book's particular style. I appreciated it when she stood her ground when she knew she was right. Paula Murphy, our longtime publicist, jumped into this new project with loads of enthusiasm. She helped translate things we couldn't even put into words about ourselves, our past and our dreams. She helped us tell our story because she knows us better than we do after working with us for 26 years. The photos throughout the book by Penny De Los Santos perfectly capture the street vendors, the daily whiz of street activity and the traditional foods the locals crave. The project was not just a job, but had personal meaning to her as well. We are indebted to Penny for sharing her great talent with us. She dug deep within herself to get the photographs and she knew when they worked. She helped bring the book's vision to life.

Thank you to this amazing team that contributed individually and as a group to make our first book so special. Thanks also to our staff at Backstreet Cafe and Hugo's. Ruben and I are overwhelmed with feelings of gratitude.

# Index of Recipes